# SNAPSHOT
# BUSINESS
# PLANNING

First Edition
© 2017 by McLean International, LLC

McLean International, LLC
18124 Wedge Parkway, #1080
Reno, Nevada 89511


Printed in the United States of America
McLean Publishing


Quantity discounts are available on bulk orders.
Contact info@McLeanInternational.com for more information on quantity orders, speaking engagements, eCourses and customized coaching programs.


ISBN: 978-0-9830529-1-3

*"Linda McLean has nailed it. This is the best combination of overview and step-by-step that will put any entrepreneur or business leader in the driver's seat. Buckle up!"*

**Jae M. Rang, MAS**
CEO and Founder, JAE associates Ltd.
Author of *Sensory Media: Discover the Way to Anchor Your Brand and Be Memorable*

*"After starting and operating 11 different businesses over 25 years, I know something about business planning… it stinks.*

*Business planning is one of those things you know you should do, but you often fail to do. I think it's because it seems so daunting. When I hear the words "business plan," I think of a 300-page 3-ring binder filled with a bunch of complicated business terms and eye-rolling word vomit sitting on a bookshelf collecting dust. The author was proud of writing it, but the business never used it. So why bother?*

*That was before I read Linda McLean's* **Snapshot Business Planning** *book. Linda simplifies the process by focusing on the key areas that will leverage your business into quick growth and profits.*

*As a business owner, entrepreneur, or CEO, you can quickly organize your thoughts and identify the biggest opportunities in your business. You probably already know what those areas are, but the day-to-day obligations have pushed it to the back of your mind. Linda's process will help you re-discover those hidden gems, bring them to the surface, and propel your organization to new heights.*

*Invest in yourself and your business. Start* **Snapshot Business Planning** *today, raise your revenues, lower your expenses, and maximize your profits. You'll be glad you did."*

**Mike Cerrone**
Serial entrepreneur

"**Snapshot Business Planning** *provides foundational systems necessary in every business! In the fast-paced world of business today, complexities challenge us at every turn. Linda McLean has taken on the complex world of business and created a simple path any of us can follow. In this book all the bases are covered: beginning with planning, on to finding and hiring talent, growth and strategy. Thank you, Linda. You have helped countless numbers of us grow beyond our imagination to achieve our wildest dreams!"*

**Erica Hill**
CEO of Keller Williams Los Angeles Coastal Region
and Keller Williams Boise Idaho

*"Just like the scenic-view signs that make taking great pictures on vacation easy, Linda McLean tells you which snapshots will give you the big picture of your business planning."*

**Pat Zaby, CCIM, CRS**
Founder, InTouch Systems
International speaker and trainer

*"Your book is an MBA course for entrepreneurs! I wish I'd had this book to read when I started my company; it would've helped me prepare so much better for the bumpy road ahead (instead of 20 years of trial and error!). All who read this book and follow your step-by-step strategy for creating a successful business will find themselves totally prepared to lead their companies to success."*

**Laura Herring**
Founder and Chairwoman emeritus, IMPACT Group,
and International Bestselling Author, *No Fear Allowed*

"Complete top-to-bottom, soup-to-nuts business planning for everyone from entrepreneurs first thinking as businesses to the most experienced business owner. Wherever you fit in the spectrum with your business, you will find nuggets and pearls with every page. Embrace Linda's wisdom."

**Michael J. Maher**

International bestselling author, *(7L) The Seven Levels of Communication: Go from Relationships to Referrals* and *The Miracle Morning for Real Estate Agents*; business strategist; and known as America's Most Referred Real Estate Professional

"Boy this book came at the right time! For the past several months I have been planning a business and struggling with the blueprint. This book got me right on a focused path and has me returning to it during different stages of my company's infancy! Thank you for writing the perfect book at the perfect time!!!"

**Pat Hiban**

International *New York Times* best-selling author, *6 Steps to 7 Figures - A Real Estate Professional's Guide to Building Wealth and Creating Your Destiny*, and host of *Pat Hiban Interviews Real Estate Rockstars*

# SNAPSHOT BUSINESS PLANNING

## 12 Quick and Easy Steps to
## Take Your Business to the Next Level

#1 International Best-Selling Author

# Linda McLean

# CONTENTS

Acknowledgements                                                    i

Foreword                                                            iii

Introduction                                                        v

CHAPTER 1:  Casting Your Vision of Success                          1

CHAPTER 2:  Identifying Your Values                                 9

CHAPTER 3:  Declaring Your Mission                                  13

CHAPTER 4:  Mind Mapping: Making Sense of the Snapshot              17

CHAPTER 5:  Financials                                              29

CHAPTER 6:  Products and Services                                   41

CHAPTER 7:  Marketing                                               47

CHAPTER 8:  Team Growth and Development                             57

CHAPTER 9:  Sales Systems                                           87

CHAPTER 10: Customer Retention                                      99

CHAPTER 11: Technology and Equipment                                105

CHAPTER 12: Office                                                  111

CHAPTER 13: Celebration                                             119

CHAPTER 14: Goal Summary and Action Steps                           125

Conclusion                                                          129

NEXT STEPS: Are You Ready for Coaching?                             131

# Acknowledgements

I am so grateful for the many talented and encouraging people who assisted in making this book a reality. To thank them all individually would be an insurmountable task. Each of you knows what role you have played, and I appreciate each of you for your unique contributions and support.

So, in no particular order, let me take a few moments to specifically recognize the following people.

I have been able to do the work I love because of all the support my husband, Scot, has given me since the beginning of my business.

My daughters, Brittany and Paige, have watched my endless hours of work and countless miles of travel over the years and always welcomed me back with open arms and eager ears, learning as they grew up and also witnessing what a woman with passion can do toward her career and quality of life.

This book would not have come to fruition without my dear friend and business associate, Amy Stoehr. Your willingness and dedication to support the final writing of this book was above and beyond the help I could have ever imagined.

Patti Knoles, your artistic vision played a pivotal role, from cover design to the complete layout. You and your team are amazing.

Gina Hayden, thank you for your discerning wisdom in all areas.

Christine Whitmarsh, your huge contribution and expertise in taking what is on my mind and in my heart, and transforming it to words on paper, is invaluable.

Al Henderson, your ability to take the whole picture and condense it into succinct, spot-on promotional copy is exceptional.

Anne Reid, thank you for your detailed editing expertise and precision for the final editing. To the ladies at Pypeline Editing, thank you for your first pass on the copy.

Mark Walker, as both my business coach and my friend, you continue to guide, nudge, and challenge me to go to my own Next Level.

Deep gratitude to the many dedicated clients who have trusted me and my team to work with you over the years. You have contributed immensely to this book – not just those mentioned by name, but each and every one of you. Thank you.

And of course, I am immensely grateful to Bob Proctor, my mentor, my friend, and a constant reminder to me to nourish my mind and hold fast to my dreams. Thank you for your encouragement and support! I'll never forget what you told me, "Linda, if you go out there and do what you really love, the money will always come." You know what? You were right.

This book is in your hands now, because of the love of God – for supporting me through His word, where I receive guidance and confirmation that all things are possible; and for His artful approach of bringing together everyone to make this book a reality.

# Foreword

When asked to write the foreword for this book, I accepted without hesitation. I've known Linda McLean for over 25 years and have watched her grow professionally into a savvy businesswoman. Oddly enough, I met her at an engagement for a banking institution I'd been hired to speak at in the late '80s. Our paths crossed again in the '90s and we've remained friends ever since.

For many, myself included, the mere mention of business planning elicits a pained expression. It's like taxes; it's something that has to get done. Personally, I'm fortunate to have a business partner in Sandy Gallagher who absolutely loves to do business planning.

I have spent most of my adult life studying the mind and why we do the things we do and why we don't do many of the things we know we should do. I travel the globe teaching people how to be more, do more and have more. In just about every seminar I conduct, I suggest that a person should seek advice from someone who has proven, by results, that they know what they're talking about. When you find this person in any given area, do exactly what they tell you to do.

Linda McLean knows what she's talking about when it comes to business planning, and she has grown her own business using the principles laid out in her book, *Snapshot Business Planning*.

After leaving the banking industry, Linda began to consult with a real estate agent who was executing 55 transactions a year. Little did he know that this woman is a master when it comes to implementing systems, business planning, and strategizing a plan of action that would allow him to grow his business exponentially. Within just a few short years, she helped him grow his business to over 400 transactions annually, becoming the #1 agent in the RE/MAX franchise worldwide.

In Napoleon Hill's classic, *Think and Grow Rich*, Hill explains, "Knowledge is power only to the extent that it's organized into a definite plan of action and directed to a definite end." This book does exactly that and is a lifesaver for anyone in business. Linda has created a business planning formula that is so straightforward – and so practical – that you'll be able to walk right through the process to create your Snapshot Business Plan. Napoleon Hill also pointed out in the chapter, Specialized Knowledge, "It pays to know how to purchase knowledge." He was right. I have followed that advice, and it has served me very well. You would be wise to as well.

When the time came for us to bring a business planning and organization expert in for one of our own seminars, Linda was the first person who came to mind. She's worked her magic with countless clients worldwide, and now you have the opportunity to use her tried-and-true system to help take your business to the Next Level.

Snapshot Business Planning is a powerful process that's easy for any business owner to take and gain a bird's eye view of their operation, then organize it for growth by identifying and setting goals in *all* areas of the business, not just one or two facets. She's helped people worldwide. Now she's going to help you.

Bob Proctor, *Co-Founder of the Proctor Gallagher Institute and International Best-Selling Author*

# Introduction

There is one thing I know about your
business already, before we even begin:
It's a diamond in the rough!

By this, I mean there is such tremendous potential just waiting to be
revealed. Like a diamond, what your business looks like now is
nothing compared to what it CAN be. It just takes chipping away all the
rough, unwanted (or unnecessary) bits to bring out the real gem inside.

And that's precisely what the Snapshot Business Planning system
does. Together, we'll examine every facet of your business, polish it all
up with the right tools and a little elbow grease.

Then when we're done, you'll have an absolutely BRILLIANT business
plan that serves as a direct path to a higher level of success. And like the
transformation from dull, rough rock to polished gemstone, your new
plan could increase the value of your business many times over!

But why me? And why the Snapshot Business Planning system in
particular?

Business planning is one of my greatest passions in life! I am often asked: why is it that a kid from the prairies of Alberta, who was raised on a farm, is so infatuated with building businesses? Good question. I guess it was as a result of the experiences I had, what I learned, and of course my amazing mentors who got me hooked.

When I was 18, it was time for me to enter the "working world." Bear in mind, I'd been working my whole life; my family owned a farm and we learned early on that work was a normal and important part of our daily lives. My brother, Gord, owned a body shop and gave me a job as receptionist while I went looking for a "real job." One day, a customer came in who happened to be a headhunter. He was impressed by the professionalism and courtesy "this young lady" demonstrated, and inquired of the shop owner (my brother) about me. In discovering I was looking for a job and this position was temporary, he immediately declared he knew of a perfect job for me at a law firm, where I'd assist the general manager.

At the law firm, I became fascinated by the detailed systems in place to prepare cases for court. I volunteered at every opportunity to help and learn more and even stayed after hours doing transcription to prepare for a possible future role as a legal secretary. My manager took me under her wing and not only mentored me in the job duties but also in the area of professional presentation. She taught me to always be thinking beyond my current circumstances, at the Next Level of where I wanted to be.

One day, I went to her to discuss how soon I could move into a legal secretary position. She told me the law firm was solid; there would be no more attorneys hired, and therefore no more positions available for me to grow into. Thank goodness she'd been grooming me all along to think bigger! It was because of this mentoring that I opened my eyes to what the Next Level might look like in my life. I was growing.

I decided to reach out to my oldest brother, Fred, who I held in high regard, as he had achieved levels of success I admired. Again, we were raised very modestly in a small town on a farm, which he left before finishing high school. Fred was a risk taker. He became the youngest real estate agent in the Province of Alberta; launched his house-building company; bought race horses; owned homes throughout the U.S. and Canada; got his pilot's license (Now *that* is another story. I flew with him once as we were flying only on gas fumes – yes, he was a risk taker!); and went on to be a national developer of apartment buildings, condominiums, and commercial properties. One thing I will never forget is when I asked Fred what his turning point was. He replied, "Reading the book *Psycho-Cybernetics* by Maxwell Maltz." He read it shortly before he wrote his real estate exam, and it changed how he viewed his potential and what he could achieve. He knew, without a doubt, he could create whatever level of success he could imagine.

So, when I shared with him that I was looking for my Next Level career, he immediately said that he had connections in the banking industry and felt confident this field would be a great step for me to advance my career, then put me in touch with key people.

And so it was that I headed into the banking business in Edmonton, Alberta, on October 3, 1977. Working up through the ranks, I wore many hats: Executive Assistant, Mortgage Lender, Commercial Lender, Auditing Assistant, and Assistant Manager of the Investments Division at the head office in Edmonton. There came a time, even though I was having a ton of fun learning and growing in my career, that the desire to start a family was overpowering the corporate-ladder climb, so after ten great years in the corporate world, my husband and I made the decision to start a family, and our first daughter, Brittany, was born. This was such a joyful time in my family. While celebrating the birth with my mom, dad, brothers, sisters, nieces, and nephews little did we know, something tragic was about to occur in our lives that altered what I thought my future would be. My mother's cancer reappeared, and within 26 days of Brittany's birth, my mother went to be with the Lord. This was a surprise to all of us, because she had purposely kept the reoccurrence of cancer to herself. We were all in shock. Being on maternity leave and grieving, I came to realize that getting back into the fast-paced world of trading in the money market and working at a head office wasn't as important to me as it once had been. After much persuading with the HR department to not go back to the head office, they reluctantly found me a great job in the local bank as the Assistant Manager of Mortgage Development.

When Scot was transferred eight months later to eastern Canada, I chose to take time getting settled in our new home rather than throwing myself back into the fast-paced, high-stress world of investment management. The timing couldn't have been better – as they say, everything works out for the good. In my position as Assistant Manager I was responsible for increasing the mortgage portfolio. I immediately set into a relationship-building marketing program with local REALTORS®. I soon met a young man who had been in business only a short time. He was doing very well, but needed help getting his business organized to reach the Next Level. He was working 24/7, he didn't have any systems, and he didn't have a clue where to start or how to change. After various lunch meetings with him where I suggested actions to take in his business – from systems to implement to leveraging through adding staff – I felt so excited about the possibilities of what he could achieve. That evening I shared with Scot how fun it was to help this young man. I had one of those "Aha" moments and declared, "This is what I want to do full time! I can make this a business!" My mind had shifted, and my actions would follow those thoughts. I was about to become an entrepreneur.

Scot nearly fell off his chair. Registering my own business was a quantum leap for us as I had been an employee with a secure job that paid very well and with great benefits. Here I was, leaping to work with a real estate agent who was still wet behind the ears. But there was something about this young man that I believed in, and the thought of helping him build his business excited me beyond what I could express. So with Scot's support (and a little trepidation), I met with an attorney friend, and we drafted up a six-month contract that simply stated if I didn't make a difference in the client's business, we would part ways after six months. From my years in the law firm and in banking, looking at all different types of businesses, I could see quite easily where companies lacked order, organization, and structure. One might show a healthy profit, but be completely out of balance outside of work. Another struggled to make ends meet, wasn't posting a profit, and never moved the business forward. Then a third (less often seen) would have it all together – healthy bottom line, systems, and staff running smoothly with the financial freedom to buy whatever was wanted, take vacations, and enjoy time with family and friends.

That's how McLean International was born – with just that one promising client. I rented a photocopier, purchased a second-hand filing cabinet, and set up my office in our basement. With a clipboard, notepaper, and pen in hand, I started work. I will never forget my first day. I asked, "Where would you like me to get started?" My client shrugged and said he had to go out on an appointment, but had checks that needed to be deposited. He opened his desk drawer and handed me well over $28,000 in uncashed commission checks. He didn't even have time to go to the bank! I leapt in, started organizing folders and creating systems so that we were highly productive with our time. I was a foreign object in the real estate office, as no one had assistants. Needless to say, people were interested in what was happening and they watched carefully. I ran back and forth from my house to his office until we graduated to an office large enough for two desks.

It was exciting for me to work with a busy, entrepreneurial individual, and with my help, he rose like a shooting star from 55 houses sold to 115 in our first year working together, and then 222 houses the following year. I kept applying what I had learned in the banking industry, focusing on the different areas of the business and working to improve each of those areas, and a couple years later he was ranked the #1 agent worldwide for RE/MAX® International. (He achieved the

#1 award a second time during the seven years I worked with him.) We always chuckled about how we built the business by writing on paper napkins over lunch. We sure worked hard, had fun, and achieved great things – we were pioneering, blazing trails in real estate. He focused on marketing and selling; I focused on operations and finance. By focusing on our strengths, we grew exponentially faster. Every year we continued to grow, and in the last year I worked with him, we sold over 400 houses. I helped him build his business in very much the same way I do with all my clients: by looking at the big picture, creating a plan with systems, strategically marketing, getting a great team together, and focusing on smart growth.

Over the years, as I continued growing McLean International, I kept fine-tuning this business-planning system. My goal was always to create a business plan that was doable for anyone, in any industry, in any-sized business. Its first model involved identifying the key parts of building a solid, successful business – the twelve steps, including eight key facets, you will soon learn about. Our business plan differs from the traditional, lengthy, extremely detailed business plan (we call them in-depth business plans). It's precisely the thought of that lengthy, in-depth plan that gets in the way of most entrepreneurs pulling together a business plan to begin with. Do you know why most entrepreneurs fail? Michael E. Gerber gets to the heart of it in his book, *The E-Myth Revisited*. Most entrepreneurs are technicians who work IN their business instead of taking the time to work ON their business, which is why we came up with a business-planning process that wasn't complex and incredibly time-consuming. We coined the phrase "Snapshot Business Plan," because ours is easy to follow and implement and generally isn't longer than a couple of pages. Our plan documents the key goals and action steps required in each facet of the business in a way that everyone in the business, from administrative staff to the CEO, can understand and therefore become invested in the outcome.

Now it's your turn to experience Next Level growth. The blueprint you are about to learn is applicable to any type of business. I have seen this work for all sizes and types of organizations worldwide, and I have complete confidence that it will work for you too!

It's true that the two MAJOR ingredients for success are to have a solid plan and to take action. I am also going to share with you many other ingredients that you will need along your road to success. By the end of this book, using the strategies my team and I use every day with our clients at McLean International, you will have a complete, doable plan of action to bring your business to the Next Level.

Before you begin, consider that throughout the entire process right thinking puts your business plan in motion – and then keeps it in motion – powering you toward results you might have only dreamed of in the past. And by following our process you will bring them into reality.

So now let's jump right in. It's time to get out our tools and our polishing cloth and uncover the brilliance lying just beneath the surface of YOUR business!

# CHAPTER ONE

# Casting Your Vision
# of Success

"**W**hat does cast a vision mean, and why do I need to do this for my business?" Great question.

· · · · · · · · · · · · · · · · · · · · · · · · · · · · · ·

*To cast a vision means to imagine what you desire to be the future for your business, and then taking what you're dreaming in your mind and forming it into a comprehensive, written statement, composed as if you have already accomplished it.*

· · · · · · · · · · · · · · · · · · · · · · · · · · · · · ·

So why do you need it? Your clear vision of success gives you direction; it dials in your focus and gives continuity to your actions.

By casting a vision and having it documented, it becomes the foundation for everyone in your business to come together and see the big picture so that their goals are aligned and they share the same vision.

Let's think of vision using a different word: DREAM. John F. Kennedy said, "The problems of the world cannot possibly be solved by skeptics or cynics whose horizons are limited by the obvious realities. We need men who can dream of things that never were and ask, 'Why not?'"

The key starting place at any point in your business is to imagine, dream, or visualize what you want your business to look like. We think in pictures, and that is a hidden secret to success. This is precisely what you are going to do in this chapter. You will identify what your ideal business looks like. If you're not normally inclined to visualize, now is the time to stay in a dream-like state and connect with the excitement of what your ideal business might look like through pictures in your mind.

Before you read any further, grab a piece of paper and pen or open up a document and start writing/typing what your business could look like five or even ten years into the future. Pull yourself up to the 10,000-foot level and look down upon your business, and then write, write, and write. Capture every thought that comes into your mind. To give you a couple of ideas where to begin, consider these areas:

- What would you like the business to be earning, and what would your net profit be?
- What would you be doing in the business?
- Who would be working with you?
- Where would the business be located?
- What services or products would you be selling?

Tap into your five senses. What do you hear and see? How do you feel? Some people choose to be very specific, even describing the marble floors of the entryway, the office furniture, and the view from the conference room. You will likely make modifications to this vision, so just let your thoughts take you where they take you. Have fun with this exercise. Remember this is YOUR vision. You don't have to share it with anyone unless you choose to do so.

We have been through the process many times of helping clients explore, tweak, and rewrite their vision. The author Wallace D. Wattles says, "One needs to first cast their vision and then wobble towards it." That is such an accurate statement, because we all set a goal and we generally make adjustments along the way to achieving the goal. What I hear Wattles saying to us is, "Don't get hung up on the crooked path you might have to take, just keep moving forward – keep wobbling!"

And one more thing, don't forget to write the date on what you just wrote. It has been enlightening for many who have done this exercise to later go back and re-read what they'd written and reflect on how far they have come.

There are so many examples of the super successful and how they used the tool of visualization to build their businesses. Here are a few:

1.  Karl Benz: As a college student in the 1860s, while riding his bicycle, he dreamed of building a "horseless carriage." He built the first automobile engine on New Year's Eve, 1878, and in 1885 his first car came to life.

2.  Mary Kay Ash: She had a vision that women could advance in business and help others to succeed while doing it. What started as an idea for a book became the business plan for Mary Kay Cosmetics!

3.  Steve Jobs: He dreamed of making a computer for the everyday person, and look where Apple has ended up!

Why do I recommend that you cast your vision out at least five years? This is far enough to allow the mind to dream. Twelve months is too close to the heart, in a place where your mind can play tricks on you. With a shorter-term vision, you may think, "There's no way I can generate so much revenue in one year!" But somehow, the idea of generating whatever your dream dollar amount is in five years makes your heart skip a beat and the exhilarating feeling of "what if?" sets in. You start to dream bigger: "I'll bet we could really do that..." and suddenly you're having fun with your vision!

As you work to craft your unique vision, here are some examples of visions that two of our clients have graciously shared.

**Vision Example #1: Graphic Design**

> *I am thrilled now that I have ten designers or more in my **Virtual Graphic Arts Department** (VGAD) company. The designers share in our core values. All are highly trained, efficient, motivated, and passionate about their work, taking initiative to bring new clients to VGAD whether they work with them or one of the other designers. Everyone works in total harmony for the good of everyone. Each designer lives a healthy balanced life, making a difference in the world through their work, their family and their community.*
>
> *Our clients come from all over the world by way of referral, and we have projects scheduled on a consistent basis with some on our waiting list. I am enjoying the $1.2 million or more with a 38% profit margin that allows me freedom to vacation with my family and friends as I desire while also pursing many personal interests. I am known as a leader in the design industry, and we have launched another division where we consult for other designers who want to own thriving design businesses. I am extremely healthy and honoring God as I do my best to fulfill His purpose in my life.*

As a result of doing Snapshot Business Planning, over three years this client not only increased her net profit by more than 20%, she also has incorporated balance and enjoys working out regularly and spending time with her family.

**Vision Example #2: Dental Practice**

*I am so happy and grateful now that I am generating $2 million or more from my ideal practice. My practice is a beautiful place where people can come and relax. They are treated with total respect, receive painless personalized care, excellent follow-up, and high-quality dental treatment. Our service and systems are geared around the patient experience being comfortable and stress-free. The client feels totally relaxed while the work is being completed. Their bookings and financial aspects of care are handled privately in consult rooms away from the reception area. The décor is light and comfortable with wonderful furniture and beautiful art on the walls. Our equipment is state of the art. We have modern technology... and our patients experience a very high level of service with a personal touch from everyone in our office. We have a team of four who are very well cross-trained to function in the clinical area as well as the administrative area. We share similar values, are professional, and operate at a very efficient level.*

*Most of the treatment rendered has at its core the neuromuscular approach:*

- *TMJ treatments*
- *Full-mouth reconstruction*
- *Smile makeovers*
- *Orthodontics including Invisalign*
- *Treatment of sleep apnea*
- *Performance Sport mouthguards*

*Fees charged are higher than the typical general practice and as a result we are really not in competition with other offices. We are in a position to help other offices with referrals of those who are not looking for what we offer and also to handle referrals from other dentists of more complex cases. With our higher profit margin, we are able to invest in other areas that will benefit our team and our community while continuing to*

**Vision Example #2: Dental Practice** *(continued)*

*invest in better equipment and stay current with up-to-date technology and training.*

*I have other dentists who share the office on days that I am not there, which expands our service days to five to six days per week. Our clients appreciate having more availability to see a dentist. The practice is very rewarding emotionally and financially. It affords me time to study, improve my skills, and be able to offer the best I can. I also have all the time I want for my family – my wife, my kids, the grandchildren, and my friends. I am living the life I have always dreamed of by also giving back to my profession by developing programs and other types of educational materials. These are well received by other dentists and help them succeed.*

When this client first cast his vision, he hadn't even secured a location to open his ideal practice. In less than 18 months, he had a fully-functional, thriving practice just as he envisioned.

Of course, you have an option. You may find corporate examples such as the following found on their company websites, which are briefer, to be more applicable to your desired vision. You may choose to do the same with your grandly-cast vision, extracting the essence, and posting on your own website:

- **Amazon.com**: Our vision is to be earth's most customer-centric company; to build a place where people can come to find and discover anything they might want to buy online.

- **Microsoft**: Create experiences that combine the magic of software with the power of Internet services across a world of devices.

- **REI**: We inspire, educate, and outfit for a lifetime of outdoor adventure and stewardship.

- **Wikipedia:** Imagine a world in which every single person is given free access to the sum of all human knowledge.

Now, take a moment and revisit the dream you wrote out at the beginning of this chapter. Stand up and re-read out loud what you wrote. You'll find power in this approach. What tweaks do you want to make to it right now? Is it specific? Does it excite you? Will your team readily understand and rally around it?

> "The problems of the world cannot possibly be solved by skeptics or cynics whose horizons are limited by the obvious realities.
> We need men who can dream of things that never were and ask, 'Why not?'" JOHN F. KENNEDY

# CHAPTER TWO

# Identifying
# Your Values

At the heart of any successful business is a clear set of core values.

. . . . . . . . . . . . . . . . . . . . . . . . . . . . . . . . . . . . .

*Core values are individual words that encapsulate*
*your principles and guide your behavior and actions.*

. . . . . . . . . . . . . . . . . . . . . . . . . . . . . . . . . . . . .

They set the tone for the company culture, clarify what you stand for, and lay a foundation upon which challenging decisions can be made with consistency and confidence. As a team, when challenges arise, each member can ask, "Is this in alignment with our values?" And when your team members truly embrace the values, their actions will align with those values. Regrettably, some businesses take on core values that are really more like aspirations – what they wish they were, not what they are. This is a quick route to eroding trust and restricting the growth of your business.

Ultimately, your business will embody no more than five core values that you and your team commit to, rally around, use as a guiding light in making decisions, and also lean on during difficult times. If you're just beginning your business, the process starts with you getting clear on your individual core values. Sit down with pen and paper right now and make a list of all the values that come to mind. Examples include success, health, freedom, faith, and integrity. Don't limit yourself on how many; let them flow. Once you have exhausted what's coming to mind, go back through your list and see if you can narrow it down to ten. Now, go back through and select the five that rise to the top as your most important.

When we take clients through our Values Clarification Exercise (available to download, along with several other valuable tools, at www.McLeanInternational.com/SBP-resources), we help individuals narrow it down to ten to start. Then, as team members identify their own individual ten, all those core values are brought together and the core five for the company can be selected.

If you already have a business, but have never done a values exercise, here's a great way to approach it. We once completed the exercise with a team of 13. Each individual identified his or her top ten, and then as a group, they shared individually and looked for the most common values. Integrity was one of the most commonly shared and highly-regarded values for this team; for them, that meant always bringing the truth to their clients and each other, even when it meant an uncomfortable conversation would follow.

At McLean International, one of our top five core values is relationships. That shows up for us in three areas:

- **Our Family.** We foster a culture that puts family first, and everyone who joins the team knows this and respects the boundaries of fellow team members. We want to ensure that we have great relationships with our families, because we know that creates personal happiness, and it spills over to the work we do as a team. Each of us asks, "What do I need to do to have a great relationship with my family?"

10

- **Our Team.** How can we foster and have better relationships with the people we work with? We take time in our team meetings to discuss personal wins and challenges as well as work ones. We dedicate part of our periodic team planning meetings to nurturing our relationships. All of this automatically spills out into the relationships we have with our clients.

- **Our Clients.** One of the cornerstones of our coaching is that we engage with our clients in a way that strengthens the relationship. We seek to understand their whole picture, and by building a strong relationship with each client, we know it will spill over into their relationships beyond coaching – their families, their co-workers, and their clients.

Establishing values and ensuring that everyone in the business understands how each one impacts their individual role is how you build your company culture. It's the second step in bringing your business to the Next Level. By determining and communicating values, you are putting a stake in the ground and saying, "This is what I believe in my business, and this is what I stand for."

# CHAPTER THREE

# Declaring Your Mission

*"Our mission is to help people reach their Next Level of living personally and professionally through strategic planning and processes."*

McLean International

Why is it important to have a Mission Statement? It's your declaration to the world of what you stand for.

. . . . . . . . . . . . . . . . . . . . . . . . . . . . . . . . . . . .

*Your Mission Statement articulates what you do, who you do it for, and how you do it.*

. . . . . . . . . . . . . . . . . . . . . . . . . . . . . . . . . . . .

A mission statement has to be three things above all: short, concise, and memorable.

- Short, as in a sentence. Our attention spans only absorb small bytes, so we need to be able to convey it in as few words as possible – think 20 or less.

- Simple, as in something a child could understand. Businesses tend to get so highbrow and verbose that their mission statements are too complicated for the average customer to wrap their mind around what the businesses really do.

- Memorable, meaning it comes to you so automatically that you don't have to read it from a piece of paper. Ideally, your business mission statement can be recited from memory by everyone in your company.

In Laurie Beth Jones' book, *The Path: Creating Your Mission Statement for Work and for Life,* she reminds us what your mission statement is NOT:

- It's not grand.
- It doesn't have to help *everyone.*
- It's not your career goal.
- It's not your to-do list.

Here are some examples of mission statements that meet the three criteria of simple, concise, and memorable:

- American Red Cross: *Our mission is to prevent and alleviate human suffering in the face of emergencies by mobilizing the power of volunteers and the generosity of donors.*

- IKEA: *Our mission is to create a better everyday life for people by offering a wide range of well-designed, functional home furnishing products at prices so low that as many people as possible will be able to afford them.*

- Juvenile Diabetes Research Foundation (JDRF): *Our mission is to find a cure for diabetes and its complications through the support of research.*

- Proctor & Gamble: *Our mission is to provide branded products and services of superior quality and value that improve the lives of the world's consumers.*

To gain some insight that can contribute to writing your mission, interview several of your past clients and customers who had a positive experience working with you. What would they tell others about their experience? This feedback can be particularly helpful in crafting your mission. If you have a team, ask them to be part of this process as well. Remember that people will help execute what they create. Take these statements into consideration as you write your mission.

**Follow these prompts to gather the data you'll want for your mission statement.**

What do you do? *(broad, and no more than a sentence)*

_____

_____

Who do you do it for? *(be specific)*

_____

_____

How do you do it? *(through…)*

_____

_____

What do clients say you helped them accomplish, or what do you want them to say?

_____

_____

_____

Reviewing what you have just written, highlight the key words and phrases that resonate with you. We're after the core of your mission.

Draft your first statement that combines those highlighted key words and phrases.

_____

_____

_____

_____

_____

_____

_____

_____

_____

_____

How can it be shorter? Cross out any extra words that unnecessarily lengthen your statement. Can you make it more concise? Pull up a thesaurus and see if alternate words strengthen it. Is it memorable? Can you commit the statement to memory with little effort? Continue to tweak it until you can.

With your vision, values, and mission completed, NOW you are ready to learn about the very powerful tool of Mind Mapping – a revolutionary, visual approach to organizing ideas into workable systems – and then we'll dive in and set goals for each facet of your business.

# CHAPTER FOUR

# Mind Mapping

Before we jump into identifying what you need to create success in all aspects of your business, let me share a simple yet powerful tool that you can use to expand on specific goals or projects; it helps you get organized and gain clarity on what is needed to achieve your goals. You may or may not choose to use this tool in each facet. Put it to work wherever you find it useful. For example, you may have a goal under your Customer Retention facet to host a client appreciation party by June 30th. What are all the areas involved (location, staffing, supplies, catering, live music, giveaways, invitations, photographer)? Mind Mapping gives you an ideal tool for pulling this all together.

According to mindmapping.net, Mind Maps have a long history, dating back to the third century. Early thinkers and philosophers used graphic designs to diagram various concepts, words, and ideas that related to a central thought.

. . . . . . . . . . . . . . . . . . . . . . . . . . . . . . . . . . . . .

*Mind Mapping is a technique for organizing thoughts and moving information from concept to*

*implementation. At its very basic definition,
a mind map is simply a diagram, a visual way of
outlining information.*

Remember in grade school when we were taught to arrange our thoughts in a very linear fashion? Most of us were taught how to use Roman-numeral outlines to organize information. We had the big Roman numerals (I., II., III.) for our main ideas. And then under each Roman numeral, we had capital ABCs, and then under that, we had numbers, then lower-case abcs, and so forth. As kids, this was the uniform, "correct" way we were taught to organize often large amounts of detailed information, usually in preparation for a larger task or project.

The problem with a system like this is that our mind simply doesn't work that way. We're not wired linearly in our beautiful brains. When attempting to process information, rather than looking at one piece at a time, our mind instead flows through a number of thoughts or ideas, many of them completely disconnected. We'll drift away from an idea or a concept over to something else, and then another idea will pop into our consciousness that attaches to a previous thought so we'll circle back again. This is the true thinking stream of entrepreneurs. With so many ideas bouncing around in their mind, they feel that they can barely grasp them all. The Mind Mapping process is a huge help in capturing all the thoughts that might be considered possibilities. By documenting, the entrepreneur can feel at peace that the idea is captured. Whew, such a relief! That peace remains, even if the Mind Map has to be changed – and it's likely it will be changed, numerous times.

Mind Mapping creates an opportunity to capture ideas as they come into your mind – no matter how they show up. It then gives you a visual format that you can return to over and over, to continue building upon those ideas. Your Mind Map is also a powerful method to share your concept with others, as they can see your stream of thinking and the tasks you've identified to achieve your goal. The end result is a more robust and complete picture of what you're trying to accomplish, thus increasing your chances of actually accomplishing it. The more clarity you have about your goals, the better the chance that you will achieve them. Mind Mapping helps to create the clarity that is required to move forward with power and precision.

**How it Works**

A Mind Map typically starts with a single concept, term, or subject matter. When we look at it from a business perspective we may have a particular area, perhaps one of the facets of the business, that we want to expand on, or it could be something very specific within that facet. We may have something as broad as marketing or more specific like a company website. The Mind Mapping procedure provides a structure and therefore a clear plan of action to **bring the idea to life.**

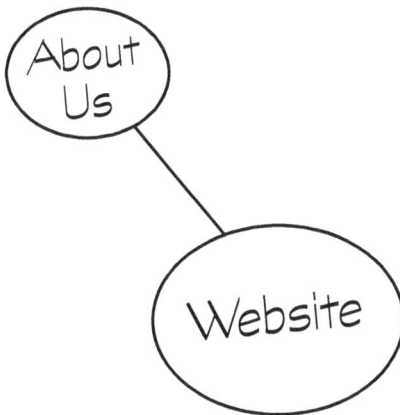

Illustration 4.1

Let's say you want to Mind Map getting a website. Your map, then, begins with the center bubble labeled Website. Next we start thinking about what's involved in a website. We realize that websites usually have an About Us section, so that goes in a smaller bubble connected to the center bubble with a straight line.

What else might we see on a website? I see the tabs across the top of my site: my mind conjures up a Home page, and then a page for Services, and now a Store. So going to our Mind Map, these become other major bubbles attached by straight lines to our central Website bubble.

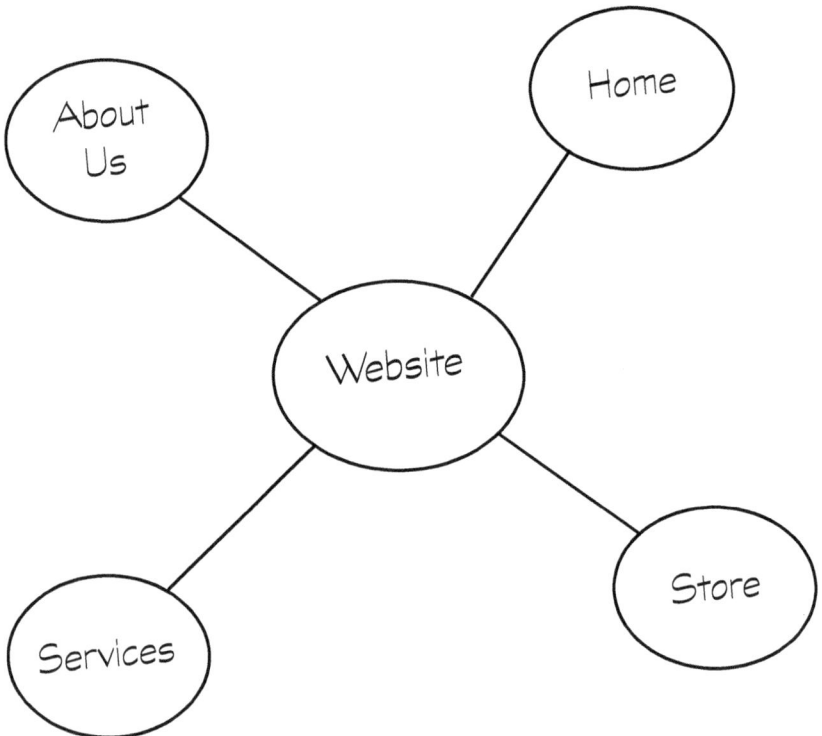

Illustration 4.2

Now our powerful mind starts wandering around the store concept, and we see in this section of our website product descriptions, packages available of multiple products, and a shopping cart to check out. On the Mind Map, I add offshoots from my Store bubble for each of these items.

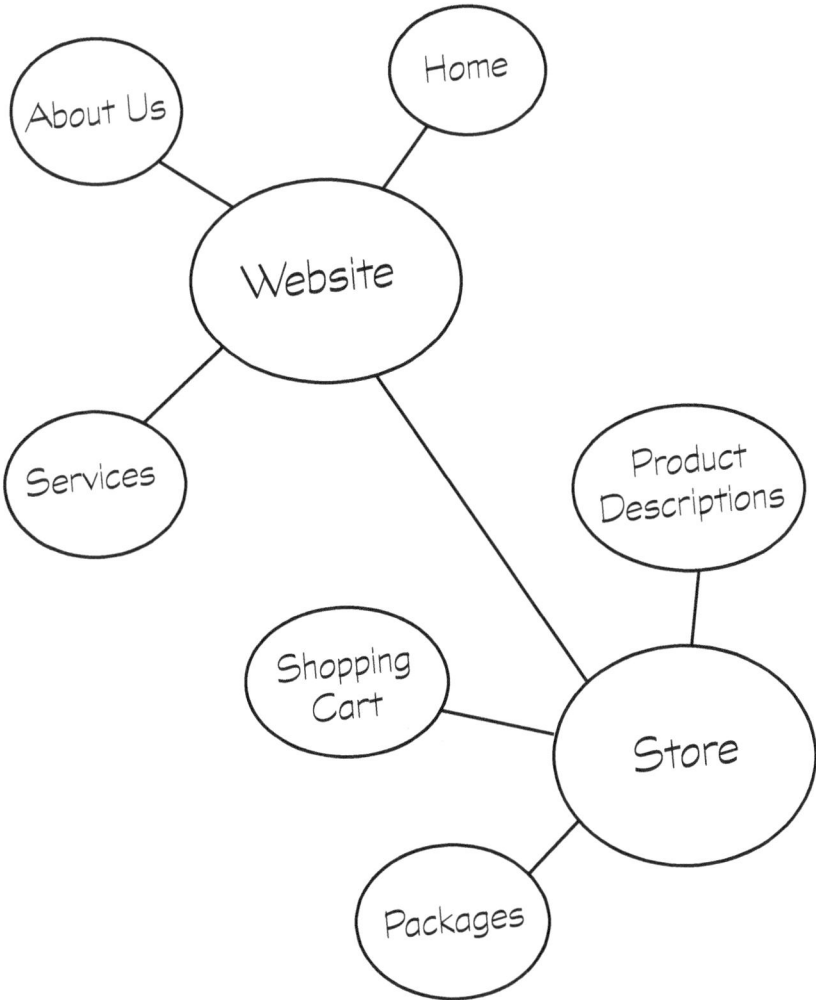

Illustration 4.3

Then, just as quickly, my nonlinear mind jumps back to the About Us bubble for whatever reason (I'm careful not to question why my mind does this; I just go with it). But with this wonderful, flexible

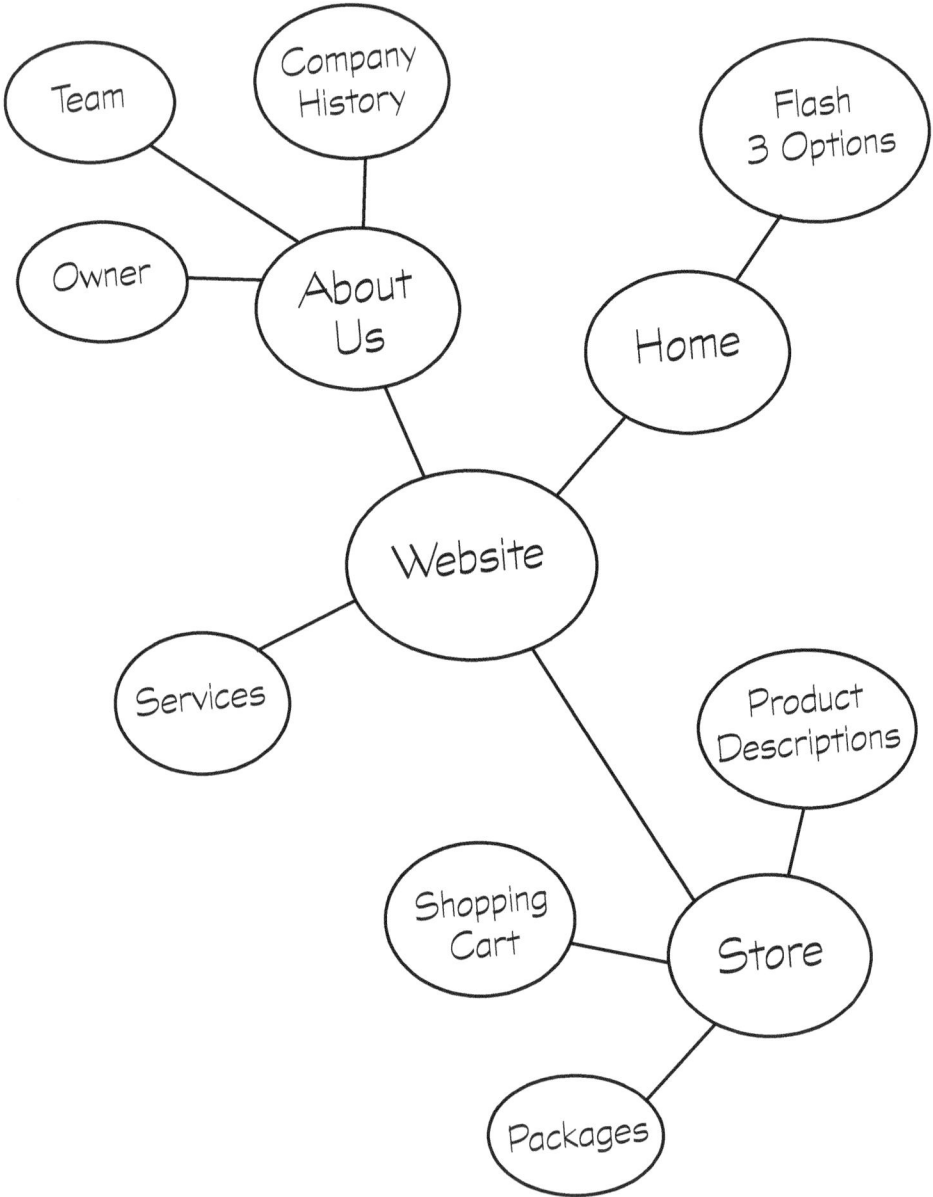

Illustration 4.4

technique I can jump back over to that arm of the Mind Map and work on that area of the website, without any disruption to what I was doing in the Store area. I start drawing new bubble offshoots from the About Us bubble: team, owner, company history. I may think of other things later, but for now I've captured what is top-of-mind for me.

Next I move to the Home bubble again, as I'm thinking I really want to have Flash installed there as an introductory visual tool. So I write an arm with Flash in a smaller bubble off Home. I note in this new bubble "3 options" because I want there to be three options above the fold on that home page.

My brain is allowed to freely flow and go wherever it might go, creating new bubbles off existing ones. Thanks to Mind Mapping, I now have the freedom to fully explore how I want my finished website to look and function, without worrying that I'm somehow "doing it wrong" when it comes to planning the project. My imagination runs free and I envision scrolling offers on each page, a Contact Us page or an interactive survey. All of these things that come to mind can be added to the Mind Map wherever it makes sense at the time to add them. If they're not connected to anything that's already there, I'm going to draw a new arm and a new bubble. If it's directly connected to something I already have there, then I'm just going to draw a branch off of that one arm. Pretty soon I have a robust model that I can go back to and add to that gives me a whole picture of what I'm trying to accomplish.

Another unique benefit of using the Mind Map is that it now extends beyond me as an individual, the leader of the company. Anyone on the team can contribute to it. I may be working on a marketing plan for past clients and customers, and I may get part of it done and then decide I want to come back to it. So I hang it up on my wall, and then as team members pass by it they may think of something I haven't thought of, visually in-spired by the bubbles already there. And if I've empowered them to participate, they can pick up a marker or a pen and write in whatever their thought is right onto that same Mind Map. They don't have to create a new section. They don't have to formalize it in an outline. When I return to it I've got the compound effect of multiple people's creativity participating in an outcome. I've invested my team in the final product from the very beginning of the project.

Think about the alternative in business, the traditional "brain-storming meeting" that many companies have. It's scheduled, there's a clear agenda, and a goal set of figuring out a certain creative problem. Everyone dutifully takes their seats around the table, legal pads and pens ready, and as the brainstorming session proceeds, each person jots down ideas on their own pad, which no one else can see. There is no compounding creative force. Mind Mapping lends to more involve-ment and with the visual aid of the map, the group is connected at a higher level to the objective.

Mind Mapping is the ultimate results-oriented brainstorming process; it is absolutely in sync with how the human brain works. It creates an ongoing atmosphere of organic, continuous brainstorming with no boundaries – great for the team, the leader, and ultimately the business!

**Mind Mapping in Action**

One of our clients owns a virtual business and hires team members worldwide. He desired to massively grow revenue, but he had no time; he needed to be freed up. His challenge was to leverage himself by teaching other people to do what he'd been doing, so that he could grow from only working in his business to becoming a leader and allocating time for working on his business. We'll explore the value of leverage in greater detail in the Team Growth and Development chapter.

We determined that he needed to develop a course to train peo-ple on his part of the model. He had been stuck in that linear mode of "traditional" step-by-step project planning and he just couldn't get beyond it. He didn't know the first step of where to begin on what was, to him, an overwhelming project. We started interviewing him, very conversationally, starting with the question: "What are the things you're going to teach others, so that they can perform what you've been doing in the organization?"

By asking that question, we freed him up to go wherever his mind took him and not down the literal, linear training route. We used Mind Mapping as a way of showing him an overview of the task, rather than getting caught up (and confused) in which detail should go first. We started with media buying, the thing he was training the other folks to do. That was our central bubble. What would a media-buying course need to entail? Through asking questions, we drew out the Mind Map for him as the thoughts were occurring to him. We were then able to zoom in further by asking what goes in the gaps.

An additional benefit of having a guide, in this case one of our coaches, involved in the Mind Mapping process, is the ability to look at it from a different perspective. Some clients have difficulty starting a Mind Map, so having a partner to capture their thoughts can be an invaluable process. We were able to say to the client, "You mentioned analytics. What specifically are you going to teach them about analytics?" The client was able to state three steps he'd take them through. Voila! The client quickly moved from task overwhelm to a flourishing Mind Map very much in progress, with three branches off that one arm that didn't exist before. Then, we kept expanding, one thought, one idea, and one bubble at a time.

A powerful question to ask when you're Mind Mapping is, "What else?" And it doesn't have to be confined to a single subject. This question simply allows the creative part of our brain to start throwing out all the valuable information it has in whatever order it deems important at that moment. Suddenly we're liberated from a structure. "What else?" is, in a way, a secret command that activates the full power of the brain.

Mind Mapping ultimately helped this once-frustrated client take a process that he was unable to accomplish in four weeks' time and have the foundation of the course written out in a matter of days. Ask yourself, what's the value to you of producing something in four days versus four weeks?

Once the Mind Map reaches a point where you feel that it's nearly completed, your next step is to prioritize what gets done first. Then, specific action steps can be decided upon to make that Mind Map become a reality.

## Your Turn

Let's take what you've learned so far and put it into practice. It's time to draw your first Mind Map! What is one time-consuming task that seems too overwhelming to tackle? Or perhaps there's an opportunity you'd like to pursue, but you're having trouble deciding where to start? That's your central bubble. Let your mind take over from here.

In business, this exercise is done best when it involves you and your team, so I highly recommend that you gather them together for this. The only tools you'll need are a large piece of paper, poster board, or white board to draw the Mind Map on, and of course, the collective brain power from you and your team. Either hang that paper up on the wall where everyone can gather around it, or lay it in the middle of the conference table where everyone can reach it to add to the Mind Map. It's important that everyone in the group gets their own marker. This is a collective exercise where all brains are considered equal.

Start by having the team agree on one item you've all wanted to implement in the business but just haven't had the time or resources to do – the most pressing thing on the "gonna do someday" list. It could be, as referred to earlier, a new website, creating a new job position in the company, a new sales system, or creating a plan for your blog. You'll most likely know you've picked a winner when most of your team says, "Yes, we need this! That's it!" Write that topic in the center of the Mind Map in a bubble.

Once you have that central topic, take three minutes where nobody is allowed to talk to each other. Everybody just starts writing in silence. They can only write on the Mind Map, adding new ideas or contributing offshoot bubbles to other people's ideas. This prevents "red-light behavior" and encourages "green-light behavior." (Red-light behavior is when people criticize or negate another's idea – shoot holes in it, if you will. Green-light behavior means the idea is shared without being contested or squashed.) Nobody says, "No, that's a bad idea," or, "Why did you put that there?" They just go! After three minutes, open up the discussion and allow them to ask each other questions. They can also continue adding to the Mind Map, this time asking, "What do you mean by this?" always with a productive, green-light focus.

Through this exercise, at the end of just ten minutes you've now developed a fairly robust system. And the best part is that it's all written down for you and your team to continue adding to and then use as a plan of action!

Think about the typical alternative for a moment: the brainstorming meeting where the leader is always "right" and everyone else is expected to turn water into wine. The pressure to succeed, to be a hero, can easily escalate into red-light behavior. For instance, one person says "How about A?" and the second person, wanting to score points with the boss, says, "Oh no, A would never work and here's why. B is much better." Nothing gets written down or accomplished and more likely than not, the first person shuts down, afraid of offering anything further because of that instant rejection they received. This is nonproductive brainstorming – the exact opposite of Mind Mapping.

The question in your business now becomes: Can you take just 15 minutes in your day? Few people feel they can spare two hours, but everyone can spare 15 minutes. Tackling a project or implementing a new system just went from being an impossible task that no one has time for to an incredibly doable task that everybody has time for. Whereas before you thought, "I don't have the time to implement more than one system a month," by using the Mind-Mapping process, you can easily now implement one system a week.

As we continue through the facets, remember Mind Mapping as a useful tool you can pull out at any time during your Snapshot Business Planning process to drill down on a specific goal or project.

# CHAPTER FIVE

# Financials

At McLean International, we lead with a focus on financials for a couple of reasons. First, most entrepreneurs shy away from them because they feel inadequate handling them. After all, if you just go make more money, don't the financials take care of themselves? Entrepreneurs are creative beings, so focusing on numbers isn't their favorite activity. Second, because many entrepreneurs don't focus on financials, they often end up spending more time and money than need be to reach their goals.

*When the financial needs of your business are met, everything else falls into place.*

Your money is your launch to freedom so that you have the flexibility to make key decisions. Yet there are two lessons kids don't typically learn in school: how to make money and how to make decisions. What happens as a result? When it comes to our money, if the topic is either not addressed or considered taboo, the message programmed into the mind is to be silent and protective about all financial matters.

As a result, people aren't always comfortable talking about money. Get comfortable because your money is the key to having the life you want!

The way in which you manage your money is directly related to how much money you will receive. This means that if you do not have your financial picture in order, you will not be in the best position to generate the most money. Many entrepreneurs know how to make lots of money, but many of them lack the management of money. As you review and respond to the various aspects of your financial picture, I encourage you to take detailed notes.

For many leaders, financials are one of the weakest parts of their business and the facet where they need the most help. If this is you, there is no reason to feel embarrassed about your current record-keeping methods (everyone has their own system, and believe me, we've seen everything), the perceived state of your financials, or any other aspect of the numbers that power your business. Don't worry about yesterday; today is a new beginning. The time is NOW to get your financials in order.

If you've not done a good job of tracking your financials in the past or if you have a brand-new business, the best way to approach this facet of your business plan is to start fresh, as if you're running a brand new company. What follows are ten key considerations that will help you paint a clear financial picture.

### 1. Select the most advantageous legal business entity.

Part of building a strong financial foundation is identifying which business entity best suits your particular set-up. Seek legal advice to determine what the right registration of your business would be. In the United States, for example, you'll explore with your accountant and attorney the benefits of being a Limited Liability Company (LLC) as opposed to an S-corp. or a C-corp. Each has its advantages as well as certain drawbacks and particular requirements. Together you'll determine what makes sense for your company. This will also create the opportunity for discussion on what changes in your business might precipitate the need to switch from one to another and help you plan and prepare for a future change instead of dealing with it after the fact.

## 2. Create, review or revise your chart of accounts

A chart of accounts is a list of categories in your business for which money is spent or received. In its entirety, it helps you organize your finances, see what's going in and out, identify any potential liabilities, and get a clear picture of the financial health of your business. If you have a current business, start by looking at what's already in place. Review your chart of accounts and make sure that they make sense and are expansive enough to cover all categories. Sometimes what makes sense in your accountant's brain doesn't line up with how your entrepreneurial mind thinks. Discuss adjustments, if necessary, so that the categories make sense to you as well as serve accounting needs.

If you're just getting started with your bookkeeping, ask your financial advisor for a place to start. If you're going to use a software like QuickBooks®, a standard chart of accounts is given during set-up and may be a great starting point for you.

## 3. Know where your revenue is being generated.

Keeping your financial facet operating positively, from a position of power and growth, is not just about generating healthy revenue; it's about having a clear system in place to track it, know it, and make informed decisions based on it. Any-sized business can make a large amount of money, but without the proper reporting of sales (and expenses), it's impossible to know what's effective – meaning profitable – and therefore, worth continuing.

When you look at your profit and loss (P&L) statement, can you see what percentage of your revenue comes from each of your products or services, or are all revenue sources lumped together into one number? Each of your revenue-generating sources should show you what percentage of your revenue it makes up. This way, you're able to evaluate the individual profitability of each product and/or service.

### 4. Track expenses as a percentage of sales.

This is important to keep track of in your reports because knowing the percentage allows you to monitor the balance of how you're spending your money. It's also useful to know, based on the type of business you have, what industry norms are. Are you way out of line in comparison to others in your field? Here's an example: service-based businesses such as real estate sales typically budget for marketing to be around eight to twelve percent of sales. In growth mode, the company may need some major marketing investments like a new website that will put marketing expenses above the standard range. Many entrepreneurs can spend a lot of money in marketing without any concept of how much of total revenue that amounts to – and with no certainty of success. If you're looking for growth in a particular category, what needs to be done to maintain profitability? What needs to happen to grow? As you learn how to interact with your numbers, you will feel more confident when you are making important business decisions.

### 5. Set a system for processing your revenue and expenses.

What system of gathering and recording expenses do you have in place to ensure that information gets recorded accurately and in a timely manner? If someone other than you is doing the recording for you, what accountability system do you have in place to ensure timely and accurate completion on their part?

You and your support person (a bookkeeper, for instance) should establish not only which numbers are being tracked and how they are being tracked, but also the method by which, when, and in what medium receipts are submitted. Also establish a clear understanding of when the reports will be prepared, when they'll be handed off to you, and when you will review them. Determine these dates with your support person, as well as your process of reports in and out, and put it in writing as an established procedure in your business.

## 6. Embrace the regular review of your numbers.

How often you review your reports will depend on the size and type of business you have and what the business requires. Some businesses need to watch cash flow every month, some every week, and others every day. Whether a "solopreneur" or a large company, at the bare minimum you should review your profit and loss and balance statements at the end of each month, and do a more in-depth mid-year review to gauge success and adjust the sails. Don't wait until it's too late to make changes!

A word of caution: don't allow anxiety about your numbers and what you *might* see to turn into a pattern of denial and undisciplined reporting habits. Let's say you know that more money has been flowing out of the business than flowing in (for whatever reason). You may start postponing your monthly P&L reviews with your bookkeeper until conditions improve. You might be thinking, "*Monthly* reviews of our P&L? I never do that until I meet with my accountant at year end to get ready for tax time!" This sort of head-in-the-sand mentality ultimately leads to a long-term pattern of sloppy reporting and potentially devastating financial repercussions! Whether your business is operating under sunny or stormy skies, it's critical to face your finances head on.

Set a deadline to review the prior month's financials by the 15th of the following month at the latest. This should include the P&L for the prior month as well as year-to-date numbers.

## 7. Evaluate your institutional expenses.

This is an area where companies often spend far more money than is necessary. For instance, your business may have a standing account to buy its paper from a specific paper supply company, yet you don't review contracts on an annual basis. How do you know if you're getting a competitive price? Put a procedure in place where an annual (or more frequent, if necessary) review is conducted to obtain bids from multiple suppliers to ensure that you are always getting the best price for the best product.

This same concept applies to many of your expenses, from cell phone packages to insurance premiums. Automatic deductions are certainly a timesaving convenience, but without diligent tracking and review, they can become significant money leaks in your bottom line. One company reviewed the timing of its interior and exterior lights being on, as well as the thermostat settings for heating and air conditioning. By simply modifying the on/off schedule, the company saved over $2,000 in expenses in a single year!

### 8. Establish a healthy reserve.

Once you've established your revenue and expenses and are able to review what your ongoing monthly cost of operating is, start building your cash reserve to cover a minimum of six months of operating expenses. Some companies hold as much as one year's worth in reserve. If you're not yet in a position to set aside the cash for a reserve, establish a line of credit as your short-term solution. You never know when something is going to pop up, whether an unforeseen expense or an investment opportunity. Having a healthy reserve gives you financial freedom.

### 9. Ensure the safety of your business.

Another important aspect of keeping your financial facet healthy is insurance. Again, this is an area where consulting with a professional is vital. Liability insurance and umbrella policies are important for many businesses. It may be time for you to explore "key man" life insurance policies as well, not only for you but also for key people in your organization.

## 10. Plan and schedule all required federal, regional, and local reporting.

Any reports that you are required to submit on a specified schedule fall under the financial umbrella of your business. Review the due dates in advance, schedule report preparations on your calendar or with your office manager or bookkeeper, and streamline their completion as much as possible. Remember many reports can be completed and submitted online. On-time filing will ensure that you avoid significant, costly penalties and late fees.

### When Is It Time to Delegate Financial Tasks?

Once you understand your strengths and limitations, there will come a time when it makes sense for someone else to take on part or all of the financial responsibilities. In the case of a large corporation, it is clear that the VP of Sales will not be responsible for the company accounting. However, in a smaller company, it's not always so clear when the bookkeeping should be delegated to someone else.

Small business owners in particular wear a lot of different hats – administrative, sales, financials, marketing, operations – and they are challenged to take off those hats and delegate to someone else. I want you to take a moment and think about how much time you, as the leader, have spent on bookkeeping when you could have been doing more dollar-productive activities or spending time enjoying fun activities you love. Does it feel like you've been wearing too many hats for too long? Here is your opportunity to create a plan for leverage!

To determine if it's time to pass the bookkeeping hat, ask yourself how much more time you would like to devote to generating revenue for your business rather than sitting down and doing the books. Track how much time you spend each month doing your books and other related financial duties. More than likely, before tracking your time, you drastically underestimated how much time you really spent on these tasks that aren't suited to your greatest talents. The universal truth for all business owners is that you will never know how much time you were actually spending in one particular role, until you hand the hat to someone else. In business, we are always learning lessons, and I have found throughout my business-coaching career, that this one is always a big Aha moment for business owners. The first thing they say after a few months is, "Why didn't I do this earlier?"

**Goal Setting for the Financial Facet of Your Business**

Now it's time to set your goals for the financial facet of your business. The goals you create will be unique to what your business needs to reach the Next Level. Based on the income numbers from your business last year, set both a realistic goal and a stretch financial goal for this year... and have fun by setting a dream goal as well! Envision the ideal level of your business: new income opportunities; consistent, high-volume clients; and a well-oiled team to support the business. By implementing goals such as offering additional products and services, leveraging yourself through a team, or shoring up your sales and marketing systems, what stretch goal are you willing to claim for yourself?

This is your time to go back to the initial dream you cast for yourself in your vision and make it tangible. When setting your stretch goal, you'll have to address the reality of what is possible and what is needed to bridge the gap between where you are and where you desire to be. The bigger the gap, the more resources, time, money, and energy you will need to invest to fill it. Take an honest look at what it realistically will take to fill the gap and then create an action plan.

We've seen some businesspeople set their stretch goal so high, that there is no realistic way they could ever reach it. Then, after they inevitably fall short, the thought of "I'm a failure" sets in, launching a destructive cycle of negative self-talk. Momentum slows, their behavior changes, and their mindset no longer matches the goals they've set.

The key in avoiding this scenario is finding that sweet spot of what you can realistically do but may have to stretch to accomplish. Perhaps, with the right resources and plan in place (and the right mindset), you can double or triple your monthly revenue goal.

This is *your* moment to dream big and then mobilize your plan of action to go after that dream! Who can dream a better life for yourself than you can?

**Sample Goals for the Financial Facet of Your Snapshot Business Plan:**

**Goal #1: Generate $500,000 in revenue this year.**

Now, map out what it will take to generate that amount of revenue.

- Currently in your business, where do you generate revenue?

- What are the opportunities for new or expanded products and services to increase that revenue?

- What can you anticipate for the coming year and in which areas? Think not only in terms of what you might charge for each product or service but also how many units of that product or service you can generate.

- What are the action steps to achieve your goal?

- Drill down deep and identify all the steps to reach this goal. What additional marketing will you require to generate the sales of this new product or service? What existing campaigns can be expanded? What should be dialed back? How often will your marketing go out and to whom? What staff will you need to support the completion of all tasks?

In this specific example, the goal is to increase revenue. Perhaps your goal is to maintain your revenue and increase your bottom line. Whatever your financial goal, it is always a choice to move forward purposefully.

**Goal #2: Set up financials in accounting software.**

We've talked about the importance of having a clear, accurate system in place that ensures your financials are easy to read. Now it's time to take action. If you already have a system in place, take some time to review your chart of accounts and ensure that the categories match your actual business operations. If you don't have a system in place, schedule a time with your assistant, bookkeeper, or financial expert to set it up.

**Goal #3: Review P&L and balance statements.**

Schedule a standing date on your calendar to review your reports, and then *keep those appointments*. The frequency of these check-ins will depend on what kind of business you have and where you are in your business. If you're just starting out, look at your financials at minimum once a month.

**Goal #4: Hire a bookkeeper.**

Sometimes goals in one facet will flow over into another facet of your business. In the Financial facet, for example, suppose a business owner realized that in order to grow and increase revenue, she would need to hire a bookkeeper. In this case, the goals from her numbers and Financial facet would flow into the Team Growth and Development facet of her Snapshot Business Plan. This example is meant to demonstrate how all the facets of a business are intertwined. When you make a decision in one, there is a ripple effect into others; everything is connected.

**Follow these steps to create customized, targeted goals for your business:**

Step 1:  Look at your ideal financial picture. What obstacles and challenges do you see in your path that would prevent that picture from coming to fruition?

**Step 2:** The answer(s) to the question above will define your goals. Identify each goal that will help you overcome those obstacles and challenges.

**Step 3:** Map out the action steps needed to achieve each goal, assign those action steps to the appropriate team member to complete them, and set a timeline with accountability checkpoints along the way.

**Step 4:** Repeat the process above as many times as needed to identify all the goals you need to create a strong financial facet of your business.

Now, let's use Mind Mapping to bring to life a financial goal as an actionable plan that you and your team can continue to develop and then, most importantly, implement. I've chosen the task we discussed in this chapter: reviewing your monthly financials. This is a critical task for all businesses, yet so many neglect to do it simply because they do not know where to begin. Therein lies the power of the Mind Map. As you can see in the following diagram, not only do you now have a clear starting point, but you also have a visual reference for all the things you need to do to accomplish this goal.

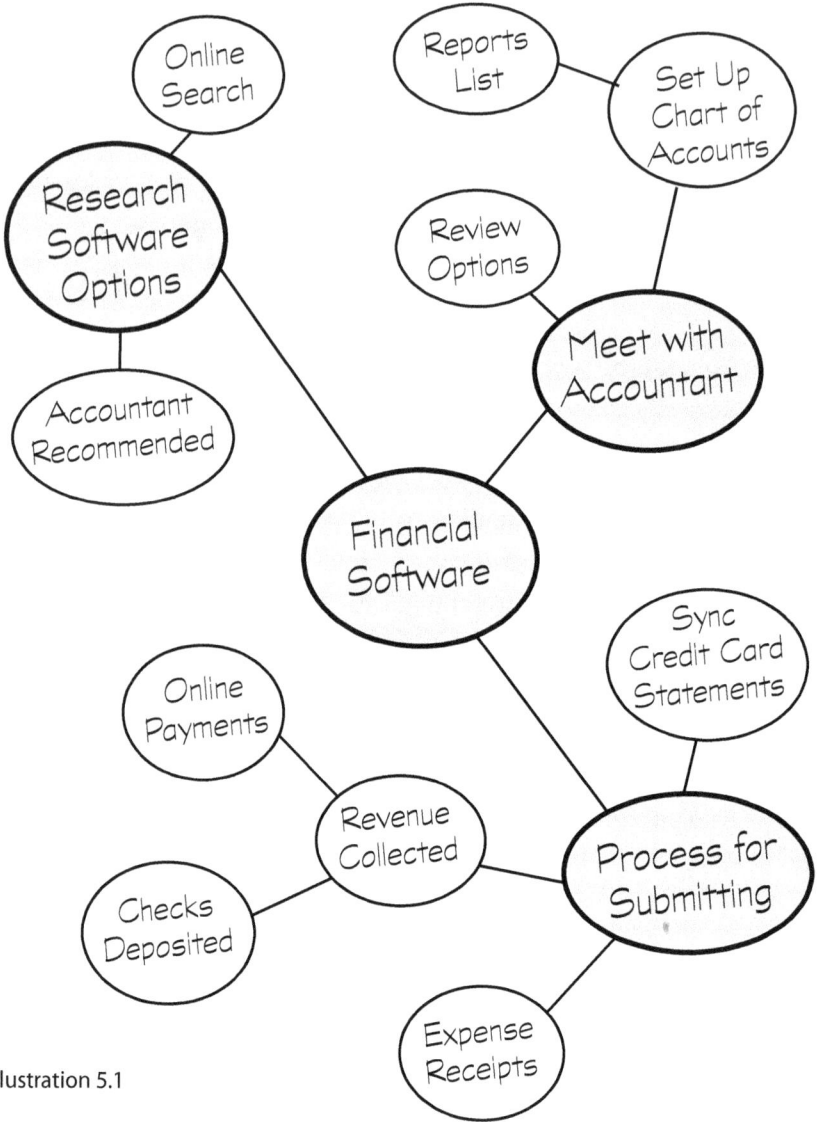

Illustration 5.1

You might have one goal or six, depending on what's working and what's not in this area. Even if everything appears to be working, don't skip over your goal planning in this facet (or any other where everything appears to be perfect). This is your chance to look for opportunities for growth and abundance! Dig deep and ask the right questions until you find the answers that will help you advance to your Next Level.

# CHAPTER SIX

# Products and Services

Now that you've completed the financial facet of your Snapshot Business Planning, it's logical to examine the very things that bring revenue into your business – your products and services. Conducting a thorough analysis of your products and services is the first step to determining your goals and creating your plan under this facet.

If you are selling products, first, write down the list of products. Beside each product answer the questions below. From each answer, determine what goal and action steps need to occur to reach the results you desire.

1. How much revenue was generated from this product this past year?

2. What was the cost to produce this product?

3. Is there a way to produce this product that would provide you with a better net profit?

4. If so, what action steps are needed to research and implement these changes?

5. What sort of an impact will there be on staffing,

warehousing, etc. as a result of changes made with this product?

6. When would you like this new product to be on your store shelves?

**Here's an example:**

---

*You've been selling a coffee mug through your business.*

1. *$10,000 was generated last year from these mug sales.*

2. *The mugs cost $6,000 total to produce.*

3. *People have been asking for a taller, wider mug. If you could find one that you can sell for the same price and produce for less, or sell for more, you could potentially increase net profit.*

4. **Action steps:**
   a. *Research a new supplier who can create the mug you want for less than what you're currently paying.*

   b. *Identify how much additional warehouse space will be required and at what cost.*

5. *Staffing will be the same. Cost will be less – $4,000 instead of $6,000 to produce. Warehouse space will increase by 100 square feet; at $10 per square foot that's $1,000 additional expense. So, the increase in net income will be $1,000.*

6. *You want the product on shelves by May 31st.*

---

Drill down and ask specific questions so you can determine what goals need to be set. Which products or services were hot this year, generating the most revenue? Which ones, numbers-wise, seemed to fizzle before they even made it out the door? Are there any improvements that can be made to any of your products or services to increase sales? Are there any new products or services that you should be rolling out in the upcoming year? What will you need to invest to do this? Are there any items that cost more to produce than the money they bring in?

Imagine you have a gift store. You see that your competitors carry decorative spoons, so you decide to do the same. After one year, when you review your numbers, you see that you're losing money because of the pretty spoons. Each spoon costs one dollar to make, is priced at two dollars, and you only sold two hundred spoons last year. In the meantime, you've been using space in your warehouse to store the spoons, paying your staff to stock them on the shelves and polish them, and paying your sales team to sell them. They could have been using their time and effort focused on other products, bringing a higher return. Was the return on this product worth it? Absolutely not! Fortunately, by taking the time to do the correct analysis, you realize this quickly and take corrective action before the business loses any more money.

Now, let's look at your business if you are providing services. The same basic process is necessary.

1.  What are the services your business provides and how much revenue did each service generate?

2.  What was the cost to deliver each service? Many companies think only about the direct cost (e.g., the consultant who delivers the service), however, all business costs must be taken into consideration – everything from a percentage of administrative support to marketing, credit card processing and other expenses. Having a well-defined list in your chart of accounts, and reading your profit and loss every month, will assist you in being aware of your cost to deliver service.

3.  Is there a way to deliver this service that would provide you with a better net profit?

4.  If so, what action steps are needed to research and implement these changes?

5. What changes would need to be implemented in the marketing of this service?

6. If you are considering adding a new service to your list, have you done the research to determine if there is a need in the market? (Refer to the Market Research paragraph that follows the Example.)

7. What sort of an impact will there be on staffing, marketing, etc., as a result of delivering this new service?

8. When would you like this new service to be available to the market?

**Example of a Goal with Action Steps:**

*This company provides coaching/consulting services to the real estate industry and wants to expand by offering a six-week, group-coaching program with an emphasis on marketing.*

| Goal: Launch Six-Week, Group-Coaching Marketing Program | Achieve by: June 30 |
|---|---|
| Action step: Survey database to see if there is a need | January 30 |
| Action step: Determine pricing and profitability of program | February 10 |
| Action step: Develop six-week layout of program | February 28 |
| Action step: Marketing layout by graphic designer | March 15 |
| Action step: Website copy for content and opt-in page | March 30 |

| Goal: Launch Six-Week, Group-Coaching Marketing Program | Achieve by: June 30 |
|---|---|
| Action step: Sales copy and follow-up copy for email blasts | April 30 |
| Action step: Registration processes identified and tested | May 15 |
| Action step: Webinar schedule with content | May 20 |
| Action step: Deliver two webinars to fill program | June 15 |
| Action step: Post-program survey | July 1 |

## Market Research

When considering what to add to your offerings, always start with what your market needs. The easiest way to find this out is to ask! And yet, so few businesses take the time to survey their market and create the opportunity to gain valuable feedback that can help them make more informed decisions. Do your best to keep your questions objective, rather than "lead your witness," so to speak. Sometimes we get so enamored with our own ideas that we pose questions naturally designed to elicit our desired response. We're after the truth here – good or bad! Include some open-ended questions to give your market a chance to share freely. If all your questions are multiple choice or yes/no questions, you'll miss an opportunity to discover some potentially powerful input.

It's also worthwhile to study what your competition is doing. While you may or may not end up offering something similar, our competitors give us insight and can also tell us what not to do. We learn from the mistakes of others as well as our own.

Once a need has been identified, you're still not ready to launch into a new product or service. It's time to do some homework. What are the costs, both fixed and variable, of creating and offering this new product or service? What will the market bear for the privilege of accessing it? How many units will you need to sell in order for it to be profitable? Does this seem like a realistic, attainable number?

Multiple facets come into play when considering a new product or service offering. Marketing will play a vital role in getting the word out on what you have available. Sales are always required. There will be a Financial ramification. And there may be the need for additional Team Growth to get the new product or service launched. Additional Office warehouse space may be required. New equipment to manufacture – you get the picture.

An additional consideration: How will the introduction of this new product or service impact your existing line? It's possible that it could enhance your other offerings, conflict with them, or even render them obsolete. It's important to make sure that the "bread and butter" offerings of your business are kept healthy! And who knows, maybe this new product or service *becomes* your new bread and butter.

Now it's time to set goals for Products and Services in your Snapshot Business Plan. Remember your key questions: What's working? What's not working? What goals need to be set to bring this area to the Next Level?

# CHAPTER SEVEN

# Marketing

I can hear some of you shouting for joy: "Hooray! Here comes the FUN facet!" People in business often associate marketing with colorful business cards, flashy website graphics, fun with Facebook, and socializing at networking events and conventions. There's nothing wrong with this at all. In fact, I encourage you to find the fun in ALL facets of your business. That's why you're in business, right? Because you are following your passion! However, it's often easy to get so swept up in that fun, excitement, and emotion that you may forget that marketing is rooted in bottom-line financials just as much as your financial facet. Those pretty business cards that you're handing out are, in reality, an expense in your business. Marketing is an investment; you're either investing or maintaining at all times.

Generally, two of the largest expenses for any company are staffing and marketing. These facets of your business also provide you with the greatest leverage. So, in order to achieve this leverage, you must get clear on the following aspects of your marketing.

Where are you spending your marketing dollars? Pull this information from two places to help you plan for the coming year. First are the actual numbers from your Profit and Loss statement (which is why the categories need to be set up and expenses entered correctly), and second is the Annual Marketing Plan Overview, which I'll walk you through now.

1.  Record all avenues of marketing on an Annual Marketing Plan Overview (see illustration 7.1) from January through December, recording the date each marketing piece will be sent, its description, its audience (who is it being sent to?), the quantity of pieces sent, and the cost. These avenues will vary depending on the nature of your business. The four main categories are as follows:

    a.  Print and Promotional: Direct mail, flyers, business cards, postcards, etc.

    b.  Internet: Email campaigns, website, blog, social media, etc.

    c.  Image Advertising: Television and radio ads, billboards, wrapped vehicles, etc.

    d.  Face-to-Face: Business networking events, client meetings, sales calls, and conferences. Events and conferences are another example of how the facets of your Snapshot Business Plan sometimes overlap. In this case, the objective of the expenditure would determine its facet. For instance, if your primary reason for attending a conference is to enhance your leadership abilities or to improve your skills, the conference falls under your Team Growth and Development facet. But if your goal for the conference is to gain new clients and make sales, include the conference expenses in your marketing plan.

Now you have a snapshot of the marketing you do for a full year. This is also beneficial for staffing purposes, as you will see at a glance what times of the year you may need additional manpower in completing and distributing the marketing materials.

2. After recording these marketing avenues individually, now you are ready to determine what is working and what is not working. How are you currently monitoring whether you are getting a Return on your Investment (ROI)?

3. Determine what avenues either need to be updated or totally revamped (perhaps sales copy or some content), and whether there are new avenues you'd like to launch in the coming year.

Regardless of the areas where you are investing your marketing dollars, it's important to give your effort time to work. Once something is implemented, changed, or tweaked, leave it for a while and give it time to work. Are you spending your time and money always changing things? All too often, impatient, over-eager entrepreneurs are so anxious to see results that they pull back their implementation of a campaign too soon. With every new piece of feedback they receive, they want to immediately change something. This kind of thinking leads to a marketing plan that is constantly in flux, with every other piece constantly being adjusted in the pursuit of instant results. Let your decisions sit. Give them space to work, and then test and track your results and act based on what is actually happening in your marketing.

4. Other considerations for your Annual Marketing Plan Overview:

   a. What do your clients want to hear?

   b. What messages are you communicating to the world through your marketing?

   c. When was the last time you had someone do a complete analysis of the effectiveness of your website?

   d. What internal tracking systems could you set up to ensure the effectiveness of your marketing?

   e. Are you getting emotionally attached to ideas without assessing whether they are the best choices for your business (e.g., *Well, John Brown did it and he's successful,*

| Marketing Plan Overview | | | | |
|---|---|---|---|---|
| Date | Distribution (Who) | Description | # | Cost |
| Jan | | | | |
| | | | | |
| | | | | |
| | | | | |
| | | | | |
| Feb | | | | |
| | | | | |
| | | | | |
| | | | | |
| | | | | |
| Mar | | | | |
| | | | | |
| | | | | |
| | | | | |
| | | | | |
| Apr | | | | |
| | | | | |
| | | | | |
| | | | | |
| | | | | |
| May | | | | |
| | | | | |
| | | | | |
| | | | | |
| | | | | |
| Jun | | | | |
| | | | | |
| | | | | |

Illustration 7.1

*so it must be a great idea for us!*)? Yes, it's important to look in your own field for ideas, looking at what successful people are doing in their marketing. However, be sure that the decisions you make as a result feel authentic for your business, your industry, and the market and that research supports them.

5.  Once you are clear on all of the above, document the goals, action steps, and desired completion dates on your Snapshot Business Plan.

You can also download our Annual Marketing Plan Overview, along with several other tools, at www.McLeanInternational.com/SBP-resources. It's the same one that we use with our clients and it will help you become aware of all the areas that fall under your marketing umbrella. Overall, the question to ask is, "What are we really doing in this facet, from the 10,000-foot level, versus just bumping along reactively, from month to month dishing out the marketing dollars without the benefit of analysis?"

**Rules of ROI**

Let's now address the big, pink elephant in the room called ROI.

*ROI, or Return On Investment, means the revenue you make above and beyond the initial investment.*

Face it – measuring our return forces us to hold our spending choices accountable, something many people prefer to avoid. When we look at the major categories of marketing, we see that some areas connect more strongly with ROI than others. Image advertising, for instance, traditionally brings in a lower ROI than a print medium like direct response marketing, because it is harder to track directly to a specific sale.

To elaborate on the role of ROI in your marketing facet, meet Brenda Do, an expert on sales-driven, direct-response copy for web and print marketing pieces. Brenda's philosophy is, "I don't just write, I write to sell." Brenda has the following words of wisdom to share:

*"There is actually a lot of misinterpretation by people in business when it comes to measuring ROI in marketing. To try and measure ROI the same way, based on the same factors across every industry and in every part of the sales cycle, is impossible. Because of this, it's easy for people to get overwhelmed by the very idea of ROI. As a result, I frequently hear misconceptions, such as someone's particular industry isn't capable of having measurable ROI.*

*Public Relations (PR) is a great example of this. Many people think that their business has no ROI on PR, but it actually does; it just takes up to a year before you see that return. The way you measure it is different depending on the industry. In PR you would look at how much top billing in a magazine is worth to you in terms of attracting leads and referrals. At the other end of the spectrum, there's the type of marketing I specialize in, direct-response mail. My methods and timeline for measuring ROI are completely different than what someone in PR would use. The bottom line is that everything has ROI. It's just measured with different variables. You also need to take into account what your goal is. Conversion for one person might be to capture an email address, and for another it may be an actual sale.*

*Something else to keep in mind when creating a system to measure ROI is that in marketing you will likely be working with several different people on all the moving pieces of a single campaign. The person who manages your social media may not be the same person who manages your direct mail or website. It's important to be aware of this so that when you're measuring the results of the campaign, each person understands how their piece fits in with the others. Each person also needs to be clear on how to measure ROI for what they're doing. Is the call to action on the direct-mail piece aligned with the social media, blog, and website messaging? How is the person answering your phones reflecting that call to action? Just like I've seen how with Snapshot Business Planning all the facets of a business interlock, the same is true in marketing – all the pieces within your marketing go together.*

*Finally, when it comes to the actual ROI measuring, I recommend that all businesses consider using a person with specialized knowledge in this area. Because to be honest, most people in business simply do not know what they're looking at when they're trying to understand their statistics. It's pretty easy to look at your Google Analytics dashboard, for example, and see all the pretty lines and numbers going up, but fail to realize what is actually being measured, how it's being measured, and what all those numbers mean for your business. It's not just about money going into the cash register; there's a lot more involved. Sometimes a low number on the front end is actually a higher profitability on the back end."*

**Tracking the Results**

After you have itemized your marketing expenditures into your marketing plan, the next step is to track those dollars and find out what is working for your business. For example, when you spend the dollars and invest the time to fly to Las Vegas for that big annual convention, are you generating clients there? What is that decision costing you in relation to the dollars it brings in?

Linda Hall, a top-producing real estate professional and one of our clients out of South Carolina, asked herself this question in regards to one particular line item of her marketing plan, a moving truck she had purchased. In real estate, it's common to purchase an unbranded box truck, decorate it with your company branding, and then use it as a moving billboard for your business. These agents frequently lend out their trucks to clients, for use at community events, or to non-profit organizations. In exchange for this exposure, they take on the liability of ownership, related organizational and scheduling tasks, and the administrative component of hiring and scheduling drivers. Just like with any other investment in your business, it requires balancing cost and liability with ROI.

In Linda Hall's case, by completing our marketing plan and using Snapshot Business Planning to find out what was working and what was not working in her marketing facet, she determined that the numbers weren't adding up. She was not receiving enough revenue-producing activity from the moving-truck purchase. Linda made the decision to sell the truck, and was pleasantly surprised (and relieved!) to find that she wasn't really missing out on anything in terms of her marketing efforts. And, even more pleasantly, she was able to reallocate the dollars previously invested in the moving truck into other areas of her marketing plan. It all began with getting clear on where she was spending her marketing dollars and evaluating what the business was getting in return.

**Making it Mesh**

Once you have evaluated the individual investments in each area of your marketing, your next step is to create a strategy that blends all the areas of your marketing together for maximum results.

- Do what works best for you.
- Do what brings in the most dollars.
- Do what is based on your values, vision, and mission.
- Do what feels authentic for you.

Richard is a real estate broker in Georgia. For years, he has thrown elaborate annual client appreciation parties: we're talking live classical music, a gourmet restaurant chef, and face painting for the kids – the whole deal – all in his backyard! An extremely social, extroverted person by nature, this type of marketing is a perfect fit for Richard. And he has the numbers to prove it. For about six months after each of his grand backyard galas, attendees continue to revel in stories about the wonderful time they had, and in the process, they refer new clients to him.

Another client of ours, Jean, is a high-energy real estate profession-al and makes similar choices in the Marketing facet of her Snapshot Business Plan. Jean used caricatures of herself and her team in all her marketing, from print to her website. This type of creativity might be considered over the top by a more introverted personality. I think of Jack, who sells luxury homes in Cape Cod. If he advertised with carica-tures and sent his clients the "bling rings" that Jean is well known for, it would be a turn-off to his clients. For Jean though, these methods of marketing are a perfect fit for her authentic personality, core values, and most important, for her target audience. She is honoring who she is and incorporating that into her marketing and it works!

**Goal Setting for the Marketing Facet of Your Business**

Get to know your marketing by writing down the answers to the following questions:

- Where can you reduce your overall marketing expenses?
- What are ways you may be able to improve your current marketing avenues for better returns?
- What are new avenues of marketing you'd like to try?
- When you look at your marketing content, what needs to be tweaked to better communicate with prospective clients?
- Always be true to your business by asking, what is working and what is not working?
- Within each avenue of your marketing, write down the specific things you want to change this year and by when.

# CHAPTER EIGHT

# Team Growth
# and Development

With your Marketing facet solidly in place, and your business on the climb as a result, it's time to ask yourself, "Is my team meeting the needs of the business?"

Our client Jennifer is a top real estate agent in the Atlanta area. Her desire to build her business and to have more time with her family has driven her to make some very smart and strategic decisions.

Jennifer came to us itching and eager to make changes to her business. She was truly receptive and willing to do the hard work, which made all the difference in her results. There were several goals that needed to be set in multiple facets. We started in Team Growth and Development.

We first determined what her business needed in the way of personnel, and then created a job description and a compensation package for each one. All candidates were given a personality assessment and values clarification exercise, so Jennifer could understand their strengths and weaknesses. This helped to quickly measure whether they'd be a fit for the job and the team and how they could best contribute. Our client ultimately found the perfect person to take on some of her workload, so she could keep directing her business.

Jennifer next started looking at revenue-producing activities that would generate more income. We looked at marketing activities to bring in more business. At this point, she had to duplicate herself in a sales role. She already had someone on board doing sales, but the fit was not right. As we worked together, she became clear about what she and her team needed, and she made the hard decision to give her employee the "gift to go." This enabled her to bring in someone who would be a better fit and produce better results for the business.

Getting this clarity about what you want and what you don't want is so important. It helps you set yourself up for success. The new people Jennifer brought on board generated double the revenue because they were engaged in the business. They're helping her take her business to the Next Level.

## Visualizing Structure

To tie in your vision of what you want to achieve for your company and your future, it's important to capture what your team will end up looking like. Whether it's three people, 30, or 300, having a visual representation of the division of roles is essential. An organizational chart maps out from a 10,000-foot view what the bigger picture of the team looks like. When you run your own business, you wear many different hats: CEO, supervisor, employee, bookkeeper, marketer, and computer expert. As your business grows, you may find those hats growing pretty heavy. Ultimately, as your business grows, positions will evolve that take tasks off your plate.

If you never create an organizational chart, you'll restrict yourself from getting the leverage you need to truly grow your business. Once it's in place, it's a tool you'll revisit at least annually to map out your next steps and to ensure you have your talent in their optimal roles on the team.

## Real Estate Agent Example

Company Name

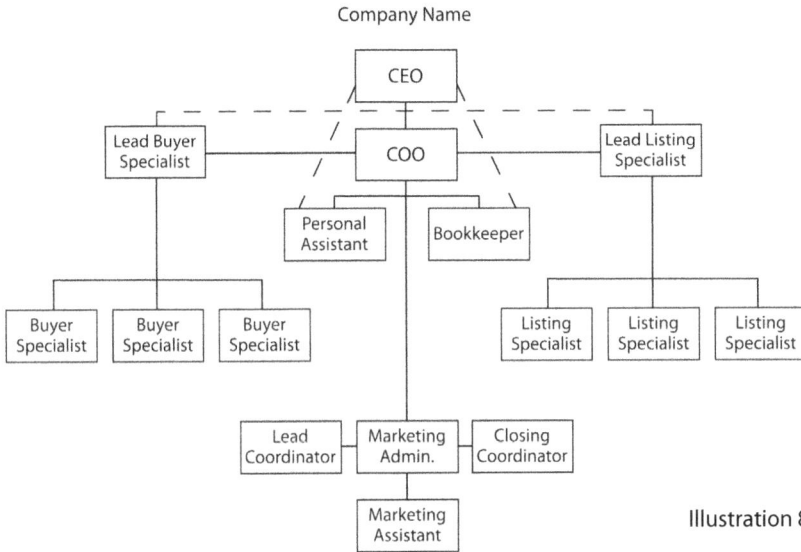

Illustration 8.1

## Evaluating

As leaders, at any given time we are adding new team members, releasing existing ones, or developing our team based on what the business needs. Determining which action to take when begins with evaluation.

## What does the business need? What is working and what is not? Which skill sets would most benefit the business?

Once you've answered these questions, you'll need to assess the people already on your team. This requires that you have an evaluation process in place, commonly known as an employee performance review.

Managerial Myth: *If I do an employee performance review, I'll need to give that person a raise, and my business can't afford that.*

This is not always the case, especially if the company has not reached its net income goals. Looking at an employee's compensation is only one area of an evaluation. Here is an evaluation process that you can follow and/or adapt to meet the needs of your own business.

**Employee Evaluation Plan:**

1.  Review the employee's initial job description from their time of hire. Now look at their current roles and responsibilities. Compare "then" with "now" and see what has changed.

2.  According to their job description, are they meeting or exceeding their roles and responsibilities? Or are they falling short?

3.  Take action based on these evaluation results.

During employee evaluations, effective communication will play an important role in making the conversation productive. You communicate in many different ways and for many different reasons. Whether you are interviewing someone, dealing with conflict, discussing how things are working in the office, or communicating with potential clients, the art of communication, and growing stronger in it, is key.

Here are some tips for effective communication that you can use as part of your employee evaluation plan:

1.  *Know your employee.* Learn about the person you are talking with. What are their current challenges? What are their real needs? Be sensitive to their behavioral characteristics and personality type. This impacts the success of your communication.

2.  *Be authentic.*

3.  Clearly communicate the *objective of the message.* What are you trying to convey? In your role as CEO, it's your responsibility to carry forward the objectives of the team with compassion.

4.  *Speak clearly.*

5.  *Be aware of your body language.* Remember you are communicating both verbally and with your body. According to studies done by UCLA Professor Albert Mehrabian, if your meeting is in person, body language is 55%, tone of voice is

38%, and content (the words) is a mere 7% of the message you are communicating.

6. *Manage your time well.* Don't ramble or allow distractions. This sends a strong message that you are respecting your time as well as theirs. You need to be properly prepared in order to accomplish this.

7. *Use your strengths,* and be aware of your weaknesses. Know yourself and your tendencies.

8. *Don't avoid communication* because it is difficult. Delaying communication because the message is not a "happy" one or the topic is uncomfortable will only delay the inevitable, and could make matters worse. Have difficult conversations as soon as possible.

**What will you do as a result of the evaluation?**

Once you have your evaluation plan in place, and are using it on a consistent basis (i.e., not just when you remember it, when it feels convenient, or when your company is in crisis), the next step is to create a plan of action that results from each evaluation.

There are three possible outcomes that can occur when evaluating your team and how well they are meeting the needs of your business:

1. Fire existing employees;

2. Hire additional people;

3. Develop the skill sets, roles, and responsibilities of your current team.

Here are some factors to consider and questions to ask when deciding which course of action is the right one for your business.

**Hold 'em, or Fold 'em**

"You got to know when to hold 'em, know when to fold 'em..." KENNY ROGERS, "THE GAMBLER"

There are many gambles in business – in fact, just starting a business can be a gamble! But knowing when to attack your systems versus your people does not have to be a guessing game. If you have a clear understanding of processes versus people when challenges arise, your plan of action will be clear.

In business, the equivalent to the "hold 'em, fold 'em" lyric could be, "there's a time to fire fast, and there's a time to hold back." It is essential to make an educated decision. The challenge you're facing as the leader might be one involving poor customer service, an accounting error, or any number of mistakes that negatively impact your business.

The first thing you need to do is take the time to gather all the information needed to make an informed decision. This is exactly where many leaders get tripped up, making an emotional decision rather than an educated one. Their perception is that somebody dropped the ball, and that person must face the consequences.

Instead of reacting this way, STOP – take a breath, and gather all the facts of the situation before responding.

Before taking action, find out:

1. Did the person who dropped the ball fully understand what was expected of them? If not, did they proactively seek to understand?

2. Did they have the proper training and procedures to perform the job/task at the level required?

3. Did they have the appropriate skill set to perform the assigned job?

> "Get the right people on the bus,
> the wrong people off the bus,
> and the right people in the right seats."
>
> JIM COLLINS, "GOOD TO GREAT"

Sometimes we inadvertently put talented people in the wrong roles, the wrong "seats on the bus" (read Jim Collins' book, *Good to Great*, for more on this concept) in relation to their skill set. Doing this sets up that person, as well as the business, for failure. The ability to recognize this mismatch will help the leader when it comes to understanding problems as they occur in the business.

**When to Fold 'Em**

Let's say that the answer to all three questions above is yes. We know that the person is super talented, experienced in this area of work, and understood the job expectations. In this case, we look at the person's disposition. What kind of attitude does the person bring to the business every day? Does he or she seem naturally prone to complaining rather than approaching their work with a positive attitude? Odds are, this person is or will become a "blamer," meaning that they tend not to accept responsibility for their own actions.

If we have done our research, ruled out any flaws in our processes, and legitimately determined that yes, the problem is indeed the person not the system, then it is time to fire fast to prevent any further negative impact on the business. I prefer the phrase "gift to go" over "you're fired!" It's saying, "You're a wonderful and talented person, but this is not a fit." Then they can go apply their talents someplace else. Everyone is a fit somewhere. By letting them go, you are empowering them to find their own way.

A coaching client out of Pennsylvania had been frustrated by his administrative person's performance for two years. "She just never seems to be able to get all her work done," our client, the business owner, told us. One of the first actions we took in this situation was to pull the employee's original job description from when she was hired seven years before, and then compared it with her current roles and responsibilities. We discovered that the needs of the business had outgrown the abilities and skill set of the employee. She was now responsible for administrative work, bookkeeping, marketing tasks, and a variety of other responsibilities across multiple facets of the business. The needs of the business had changed, but our client was fearful of letting her go.

Managers and owners in situations like this have the tendency to live within the problem, denying the potential harm being done to the company, rather than facing facts and finding the courage to give the gift to go. Letting an employee go is rarely a pleasant experience in business. There is the difficult conversation with the person, as well as the daunting task of replacing her and training a new person. However, as we pointed out to our client, keeping someone who is not a good fit for what the business needs can be an equally-unpleasant experience for the employee, as well as the rest of the team, and even the company's clients. Customers have a tendency to sense when something is "off" in a business; the tension is palpable. A bad fit in a business can grow into the giant pink elephant in the room that everyone becomes painfully aware of. It is the sole responsibility of the leader to step up and have the courage to deal with the situation without delay.

In the case of this client, once he did "confront the elephant," he uncovered all the things in the business that were either left undone or weren't done properly in the two years that he had been living in the problem. Fortunately there was no permanent damage done to the business. But if he had made the choice from day one to constantly evaluate what the business needed, take an objective view of how his team was meeting those needs, and take action quickly, those two years of frustration could have been avoided.

### Hiring

Let's say that you have evaluated the needs in your Team Growth and Development facet and the answer is – a bigger team! For larger businesses, this is typically a constant need, especially during periods of growth. In fact, I recommend that all businesses maintain a mindset of constant recruiting. Make it your practice to constantly seek talent that fits the needs and values of your business, rather than waiting until the last minute and rushing the recruiting process.

Team growth is also a frequent need in small- to mid-sized businesses. Craig, a business-coaching client, was experiencing a period of extremely rapid growth in his real estate company. Once a one-person shop, a shift for the better in the economy along with a major focus on direct-response marketing suddenly created more customer demand than he himself could handle. Craig enlisted our coaching services to help him manage the growth effectively by shoring up all facets of his business, starting with growing a team.

As I've mentioned before, with Snapshot Business Planning some facets will require more work and more goal setting than others. In Craig's case, we spent many of his coaching sessions working on the Team Growth and Development facet. From asking the key question, "What does the business need?", we determined that in order to manage the onslaught of new customers, he would need to recruit, hire, train, and develop administrative assistants along with additional sales agents. Throughout the course of a year, Craig faced a variety of challenges in this facet. He first had to find employees with the right skill sets and core values to match the needs of the business. Then, as the leader, he dealt with on-the-job learning curves with having a staff.

By year's end, Craig told me that he felt like he'd undergone several years' worth of human resources and management training, all in twelve months! But most important, he was able to allow his business to grow to meet the demand of all his new customers and create a stable company infrastructure for exponential growth.

Many of our small-business clients come to us saying, "I'm getting really busy! I need to hire someone!" So how do you go about finding the next member of your team and making sure he or she is a good fit?

I usually start by asking the client, "What are the specific things that need to come off your plate? Which hats don't fit very well? What are the first things you'd love to delegate to someone else?"

These questions acknowledge the fact that as the leader, it is not your job to be good at everything in the business. Do what you most enjoy and what you do best! It's your job to perform the tasks where you have the most passion and skill, and assemble a team of individuals that meets the other needs of the business. Hiring a team gives you the freedom to do what you love the most often.

Build your team with an eye on leveraging your own strengths and passions and identify where in your business you can add value. Recruit new team members to handle some of the tasks you don't have the time or experience to do well. By focusing not just on the business needs, but also on what you personally need, you can move more effectively in the direction of your goals.

Once you're clear on the tasks you need done, the next step is to formulate them into a job description. After all, you can't ask for something if you don't know what you want! You'll need to assign a monetary value to this job – a pay rate that honors your company budget as well as one that is competitive with your local market's offerings, is commensurate with the person's level of experience, and is reasonable for the tasks you're asking to have completed. As nice as it would be to hire your ideal employee at $65 an hour, if you can only afford $15, you'll have to adjust your strategy. The goal is to get the right team members performing the tasks that add the most value, which will ultimately add the most revenue to the business.

Hiring the wrong person can cost a tremendous amount of money. 41% of companies surveyed report that a bad hire has cost them $25,000 or more!

Now that you clearly know what you need, post your job description online. Also talk to your sphere of influence and your friends and contacts for referrals. You might even consider engaging a staffing agency. As you receive resumes and recommendations, compare each person to that job description to determine whether they can offer what the business needs. Commit to this process, and over time you will find a good fit.

As you're going through the hiring process, a word of caution: think long and hard on hiring close friends, family members, or friends of family. In small businesses, there are often family members involved, and that's fine. Be clear that hiring through your family adds extra challenges, because you may feel pressured to hire someone who isn't a good fit or to keep someone out of a sense of obligation, even if they aren't working out.

One of our clients was extremely busy and had decided he needed someone to do his computer work. He told a friend, who said his daughter was looking for a job. So he hired her without going through any sort of vetting process. Guess what? She spent more time on Facebook and doing her nails than she did working. She didn't know any of his software programs, but he found it very awkward to fire her because of the close relationship he had with his friend. If he had gone into the process with a clear plan and a job description, he would have been able to interview his friend's daughter, like any other job applicant, and would have seen from the start that she wasn't a good fit.

These situations unfortunately happen over and over because too many business owners lack a clear hiring process. If you've made a bad hiring decision, you're not alone. But now you've seen that making future mistakes is entirely preventable.

If you come into the process knowing exactly what you want, you'll be able to see clearly how your new team member will fit into the solid foundation you're building for your business.

### Developing Your Team

We began this facet of your Snapshot Business Plan by asking: "Is your team meeting the needs of the business?" As a result of answering that question, and the evaluating process, you determined whether you needed to fire, hire and/or further develop your team. You then learned strategies for offering the "gift to go" and hiring slowly and with purpose. Now let's talk about the keys to developing your people and some tools for team growth and development that you can use in your business.

Whether you are the business owner, a VP, supervisor, or manager, you are the CEO; therefore, you work for your team. It is your job to help them reach their greatest potential. As discussed earlier, it's essential to take the time to really look at and evaluate each of your employees to determine their strengths and weaknesses and then create a plan of development that maximizes strengths and offsets weaknesses. For example, does your employee need individual coaching? Closer accountability? Additional skills training? Is the person working enough hours? Too many? Document the plans you have for each person's individual strategy (visit www.McLeanInternational.com/SBP-resources to download a package of resources that includes a handy Development Plan form). By the way, you should be doing one for yourself as well!

Developing your people requires constant evaluations to answer these questions, followed by creating plans of action. How can the business support the development needs of each employee? How can you help each person rise up and develop in his or her role at the next level? It is your job as the leader to help them get better, or let them go.

As you read each of the following sections aimed at helping you develop your people, I want you to continue asking yourself our key Snapshot Business Planning questions: What does the business need? What's working and what is not? What will you do as a result?

**Accountability**

> "Accountability breeds response-ability."
>
> STEPHEN R. COVEY

Accountability is an important core value in businesses of all types and sizes. However, if viewed as a standalone concept, the idea of accountability runs the risk of becoming nothing more than lip service – all talk but no action to make it stick. Creating an accountability system establishes a concrete foundation of communication, so your team members have total clarity on what is expected of them and the consequences of failing to deliver on those expectations.

Following this step-by-step process to establish a system of accountability in your business will enable you to move your company or organization to the Next Level.

### Step 1: Outline Your Expectations

The clearer your policies and procedures are from day one, the easier it will be for your team to understand exactly what is expected of them and then follow through. Each team member should always have a current, detailed job description that includes his or her position requirements and key responsibilities. Both areas of the description will evolve as the team member grows professionally along with the business. Therefore, it's a good idea to schedule times to periodically review each person's job description and ensure that requirements and expectations are always current.

### Step 2: Set Your Checkpoints

Team members thrive with structure and accountability. Put a system in place so that every time a new responsibility or task is assigned, there is a timeline attached for completion and a specific way to submit progress reports. For instance, on my team we use Dropbox® to post, share and update our to-do lists. Our policy is that by noon every Friday, each team member will update their to-do lists with progress notes on each task or project. This is just one example of how technology can be used to create checkpoints. No matter which system of checkpoints you choose, be sure that you put your process in writing so each team member is clear on expectations.

## Step 3: Review the Results

Inspect what you expect! As the leader, you must also set check-points to review all those progress reports that your team members are so diligently transmitting.

For instance, your team members send you their reports by Fridays at noon. Your personal accountability checkpoint says that you will review all reports by Mondays at 5 p.m., and your weekly evaluation meetings with team members will be on Tuesdays from 8 a.m. to 10 a.m. During the meetings, address accountability issues such as missed deadlines or incomplete tasks, as well as blocks or unanswered questions. There might be a situation where the person is stuck in the middle of a task and needs clarification or additional resources in order to complete it. Or perhaps, the person is not prioritizing her time or not following the system or procedure in place for this specific task. This is the time where you open the communication lines between leader and team member and make sure that everyone is clear on processes, expectations and deadlines. Silence can have destructive consequences for the business.

## Step 4: Be Clear on Consequences

No blueprint for accountability (like the one you're creating by following these steps) can be complete without consequences. What do you do if someone says they're going to get something done multiple times and ultimately it does not happen? This is often the most challenging situation for a leader to encounter. Your first instinct may be to proclaim, "You're fired!" To avoid such drastic and knee-jerk measures, have a procedure in place for yourself as the leader in which you document all the positive things your people do, as well as the negative. In my business, I use a simple document called a *Performance Note* where I can easily jot down the date, the team member's name and the action (in brief; no essay required). That way if the same person drops the ball at any point, I have a documented system for seeing the big picture, which prevents me from just zeroing in only on the particular mistake. This is an excellent way of tracking the overall performance of each team member and quickly identifying any problematic patterns.

## When to Hold 'Em

Answering the three questions posed earlier, you discover that despite a certain person's assurances that they could absolutely do this job, they simply do not have the right skill set. Perhaps, prior to having a solid hiring practice in place, you rushed out and hired too quickly, or maybe it took this situation to truly reveal this person's strengths and weaknesses. No matter what the reason, as the leader, you now have the opportunity to realign and improve your systems flow for better outcomes.

In a way, unfortunate situations like this can be blessings in disguise. Now that you have identified room for improvement, you are able to sit back, evaluate what's working and what's not, determine how your system should work, make the necessary changes, and then share the results with your people.

Take note of the cycle we have identified here: problem, information gathering, determining the root cause, defining an improved system, and communicating it to your team. This is another problem-solving tool to take your business to the Next Level!

## Tips for Challenging Conversations

Whether you are challenging your team on their follow-through ("hold 'em") or giving an employee the gift to go ("fold 'em"), the approach is the same. These tips should help you in your preparation for this type of encounter:

1. Get clear on why you are having the conversation.

2. Understand you *and* them. Be aware of the personalities (some

people are more sensitive and require a softer approach, while others appreciate fast and to-the-point comments). Adapt your behavior accordingly.

3. Be clear about how/where you are going to have the conversation. Privacy is imperative to honor yourself and the individual or group. (Texting is not okay for difficult conversations!) If you are addressing an individual's challenges, don't do it in front of a group!

4. Set aside enough time for the interaction, but not too much time. Setting aside too much time can result in the situation becoming unnecessarily uncomfortable. Be clear on how you will bring the conversation to an end and how things are left at that time.

5. Be objective. Remove your emotions from the situation.

6. Honor the other person. Speak in a respectful tone. It does not matter if he or she is your employee; they deserve respect just as you do.

7. Listen attentively to their response. Be sensitive to what the conversation brings up for them.

8. Follow up with a written version of the conversation you had.

Ultimately, when a performance lapse occurs, it is your job as the leader to acknowledge the error, help the person course-correct, record your performance notes, and move on. Establishing a system of accountability like this is a valuable tool in your business.

## DISC Teams and Values® Personality Assessment

A big part of taking your business to the Next Level includes understanding yourself and your people at a deeper level. You can understand more about who you are and why you make the choices you do by assessing your behavioral patterns.

Behavioral patterns are indicators of where our strengths and weaknesses (or "limitations" as I call them) lie. They are separated into four quadrants: Dominant, Influential, Steady, and Compliant (DISC). The study of these patterns dates back as far as Hippocrates (the great physician in 400 B.C.). Even back then, they used essentially the same four quadrants to analyze people's overall behavioral tendencies. The same is true today for many of the behavioral assessments on the market.

The DISC Teams and Values® assessment ("DISC" for short) provides insight into our preferred communication style and digs deeper into the four quadrants, establishing a base for improved communication and production levels. This particular version of DISC is our preferred tool because it also assesses how we function in a group and indicates what we truly value and what internally motivates us. If you and your team have never taken an assessment like this before, it is an ideal starting point to evaluate your respective personality styles. Contact us at info@mcleaninternational.com if you'd like to take the DISC Teams and Values Assessment.

This assessment will categorize you and your team members into one of four major personality styles that correlate with the previously mentioned quadrants: Dominant, Influential, Steady, and Compliant, and it produces a score across each of the four quadrants. Because most of us aren't just one personality type, it will allow you to see the combination of styles you possess and how to use them to your advantage as the business leader.

## DOMINANT/DRIVEN

*Individuals who are dominant tend to be the doers. They are task-oriented and outspoken. The positive aspects of this type of person are that they are independent, persistent, and direct. They can come across as fearless, busy, and very energetic. On the negative side, they can be demanding and at times tend to focus on their own goals rather than the wants and needs of others. This can often come across as bossy and egotistical, depending on your perception of the situation. These are people who can undoubtedly get things done, but they sometimes steamroll over those around them in the process. Many CEOs, business owners, and professional athletes have this personality style.*

## INFLUENTIAL/OPTIMISTIC

*This personality type is what you may think of as creative or the natural-born salesperson. They naturally and comfortably influence those around them. They are very social with many friends and tend to be optimistic and future-oriented. They focus on people rather than things or tasks. Quite frankly, these people are fun magnets! The party starts when they walk into the room. Unfortunately, they also tend to be poor time managers and can get easily distracted. If you have a friend or family member with this personality, then you have probably experienced them showing up late – fashionably, right? Many artists, salespeople, and marketing/PR people tend to have this personality style.*

. . . . . . . . . . . . . . . . . . . . . . . . . . . . . .

## STEADY/SUPPORTIVE

This type of person tends to stay in the background and is the solid foundation for others. They are naturally supportive and are good at keeping the peace, staying organized and implementing solutions. They offer a strong shoulder to cry on and wise counsel. They tend to only have a few friends, but those relationships are strong. On the other hand, they also tend to be shy and avoid conflict. They don't like uncertainty and can get very stressed in times of change. Often people with this type of personality will take on jobs such as counseling, nursing, administrative, teaching, or other nurturing roles.

. . . . . . . . . . . . . . . . . . . . . . . . . . . . . .

## COMPLIANT/CORRECT

This type of person tends to be a perfectionist. Both conscientious and careful, they are critical thinkers and factor logic into all situations. They are very organized and follow rules to the letter. They are very private but have a few good friends. They value consistency, quality, trust, and integrity. Sometimes this type of personality is described as cold, quiet, or aloof. This is because they don't show emotion as freely as others do and are very private, not sharing details about their lives that other people don't think twice about sharing.

. . . . . . . . . . . . . . . . . . . . . . . . . . . . . .

From these four types, we can make some broad generalizations to what personality type certain behaviors fall into. In the chart that follows, you'll find helpful summary items to clue you in to the personality types. Keep a copy of this handy, perhaps by your phone, as a quick reference. Download a color version of this reference chart at www.McLeanInternational.com/SBP-resources.

| **D**<br>Director<br>WHAT? | **I**<br>Socializer<br>WHO? | **S**<br>Supporter<br>WHY? | **C**<br>Thinker<br>HOW? |
|---|---|---|---|
| *Want to make money, save time, be more efficient* | Want to have fun, talk about themselves | *Want security, safety, sense of belonging* | *Want practicality, logic, fairness, systematic approach* |
| *Be short and to the point – closed questions* | Add humor; don't labor on details | *Ask for their opinion & feelings – open-ended questions* | *Give facts, documentation, data, printouts* |
| SEEKS:<br>*Productivity, bottom line* | SEEKS:<br>Recognition, fun | SEEKS:<br>*Acceptance* | SEEKS:<br>*Accuracy, consistency* |
| FEARS:<br>*Being taken advantage of* | FEARS:<br>Loss of prestige | FEARS:<br>*Sudden change* | FEARS:<br>*Criticism of work* |

Illustration 8.2

I realize that you may be thinking, so what? What do a four-quadrant system from 400 B.C. and a big chart have to do with changing my behaviors and how I interact with my team? It helps, because it allows you to identify your own personality type and also identify the personalities of those around you. We tend to attract people in our lives who balance us. For example, if you are a dominant or compliant personality, you might have a spouse, employees, or friends who are Influential or Steady types of people. This promotes balance, but also sets up the potential for conflict.

I have a client – we'll call her Marta – who has a very dominant personality. She can get almost any project from point A to point B very efficiently and effectively. Her business partner, Susan, is quite different. Susan is a bubbly, creative type and drives Marta crazy at times, because she is so unorganized and never makes it to a meeting on time. But their partnership works. I asked Marta why their partnership works so well.

*"Years ago, I had another business partner in a venture that eventually failed. She had the same personality type as Susan and honestly, it drove me crazy. I kept expecting my partner to change and be like me, and the fact that she couldn't resulted in tremendous stress and problems. After the partnership dissolved, I realized that I missed her great creativity and positive energy. I had to take responsibility for the fact that I didn't know how to work with her personality – to take the good and let the bad go. We should have set up specific tasks and responsibilities drawing on our strengths.*

*When I started my current business I realized I needed someone with that creative and positive mindset. My new partner, Susan, has that personality, and while it can still drive me crazy when she shows up fifteen minutes late sometimes, I know that the creativity she brings to our business is vital. I'm committed to working hard to make this partnership work as well as possible. With the knowledge of DISC, we know how to communicate better to achieve the desired result."*

Marta's balanced perspective shows the tremendous strides that can be made when you learn to work with the various personalities and capitalize on their good qualities while counterbalancing any conflicts. This one idea can improve your relationships and your life today, just by becoming aware and using some simple techniques to work with a particular personality type rather than against it.

## Techniques

### Dominant/Driven

If you are dealing with a dominant personality type in your life or on your team, rather than getting frustrated or intimidated, make an effort to understand what motivates them and where they are coming from. For example, when you discuss a particular issue, stick to the facts rather than focusing on the people involved. Talking about the personalities versus the facts, will be viewed as "drama," which this type tends to tune out. Keep in mind that dominant people are bullet-point people. They want the facts without clutter and want to know how you can help them get from one point to the next with the fewest detours. They want to succeed and they want to conquer, so show them how you can help them do that.

### Influential/Optimistic

Influential people need to make a personal connection. They can't be rushed into the facts until they have chatted for a bit. They need encouragement to motivate them to complete tasks and set and meet clearly-defined deadlines, rather than ultimatums. They need for you to listen to them; take heart that your patience will be rewarded. Know up front that they may not be all that organized or strong with follow-through. If you have that expectation, as Marta did with her first partner, then you will be disappointed. Approach this personality with caring, acceptance, positive reinforcement and an understanding of what will work. Keep feedback lighthearted and give them the space to have fun!

### Steady/Supportive

Steady people can be resistant to change, so any situation requiring them to change or alter their thinking must be approached with caution and supported with reassurance. They need for others to take a genuine interest in them as people and have little use for shallow relationships. They do not like to be rushed or forced to make decisions immediately. Patience is required as you allow them to adjust to the idea of change before committing to it, but it is the best way to get them on board with new ideas. These individuals respond well to those who take note of their accomplishments and abilities, and they demonstrate incredible loyalty and commitment in return.

*Compliant/Correct*

Compliant people do not like surprises. Their world is one of habit and expectations; unexpected circumstances tend to be met with great resistance. In dealing with this type of personality, communicate as much information up front as possible. Present facts and be prepared as they do not respond to someone shooting from the hip without concrete backup. If you have a conflict, be very specific and focus on the facts rather than the emotion of the event. With this type you must be persistent, diplomatic, and patient.

Your first and most important step in studying the DISC is self-awareness. As you study each of the personality types, consider how your own behaviors indicate your dominant style. With this awareness, you'll start to see where past failed communications may have been fueled by the difference in your style and that of the person you were trying to interact with. What can you do to change your behaviors to better accommodate others?

We specifically use the DISC TEAMS and Values Assessment, one that we have been certified in, for its amazing depth and comprehensive information. It provides even more knowledge about the people on your team that helps you determine how to communicate, assign tasks and create a higher level of productivity and profitability in the company. Think of an iceberg – what you see above the water is the DISC; the Values is the substantial portion that exists below the surface. It tells us so much more about ourselves and our behavior.

The Values Profile, in a graph, represents one's internal motivation – that individual's life ideals. What needs have to be met within a person so that they want to stay with the company longer term? If an individual's essential needs aren't met, that person will seek a new environment. The four key areas, Loyalty, Equality, Justice, and Personal Freedom shed light on this.

The TEAMS Profile, also represented by a graph, tells us the ideal preference of what an individual likes to do. This isn't about skill – it's about desire. There are five different roles that people have to perform in a company – Theorist, Executor, Analyzer, Manager and Strategist. If a person loves to analyze, for example, it makes sense to put her in a role where she gets to utilize that passion. This person will be excited about what she does to contribute, and will likely deliver a better end result. Whether you are looking at hiring someone or at putting together a personal development plan for the team member, TEAMS and Values gives you invaluable insight to position each member of your team for optimal happiness and unification in the company.

For more information or to order a profile for yourself, contact info@mcleaninternational.com.

For one-on-one support and training on behavioral patterns, and to take an assessment, contact us at info@McLeanInternational.com, and we will be happy to help. The key is finding ways to learn more about yourself from an objective standpoint.

Once you have a good understanding of the four behavioral characteristics, you can operate more effectively and communicate with others better. This is yet another step toward your Next Level of business living as well as a leap toward experiencing better overall outcomes in your life.

**Goal Alignment**

Now that you understand, via DISC, your own personality style as well as the styles of your team members, I want to introduce you to one method of aligning all those different personalities around the goals and needs of the business.

I'm about to let you in on a company secret. I love sharing this organizational tidbit. At McLean International we have an internal name for our team: Team Tiger. Creating an internal name for your company helps strengthen the connection your team members have with your objectives and overall mission.

People attach an identity to an internal company name, which is sometimes tricky to do with an actual company name. For instance, my personal name happens to be a part of the company name – McLean International. So it would be easy for my team to think: "I'm working for Linda. I'm doing this for Linda. Linda is paying me." The reality is, when we're working as a team we are working for the same common goal rather than "for Linda." Therefore, creating an internal company name helps us think in those terms: "I'm working for Tiger." Tiger becomes the living creature at the heart of the company. And by choosing an animal name as our identity, it becomes easy to remember that the company must be fed, cared for, and nurtured so it can grow healthy and strong. I like to remind my team that everything we do, all those tasks and projects have one common goal – keeping Tiger healthy! This instantly unites the team members behind a living, breathing mission.

There are several different ways to come up with your own version of Team Tiger. The process is a collaborative exercise and an excellent opportunity to review your mission, goals, and objectives while selecting an internal name that reflects them. Does it have to be an animal? Absolutely not. Although I frequently see people select animal names because, as I mentioned in regards to Tiger, animals are moving, surviving, living organisms, just like your company.

Having an internal name is applicable to companies of all levels and sizes, but if you have 30 or fewer people (more might get unmanageable), here is an exercise you can do with your team to help you choose that identity:

Select one person to coordinate the process. This individual will moderate, making notes of suggestions on a white board or flip chart and tallying the votes as you work to choose your internal name.

Start by asking each team member to come up with two different names that they feel reflect your company's identity.

From there, create a process of elimination wherein the laundry list of names is eventually whittled down to one final name – your new internal name.

As you work to do this, encourage a respectful debate among your team members, giving each person a chance to describe and defend their choice (similar to the Mind Mapping process). Be sure and lay down the ground rules for a respectful debate ahead of time, so that each person feels that their voice is being heard (i.e. no red-lighting the suggestions). This discussion in particular will help your team members further understand the mission and the company as a whole.

I would encourage you to make a date with your team today, and follow this step-by-step team naming process I have outlined. Once you have agreed on a name, here's what to do next.

**Follow the Leader**

When you want people to follow you, adapt and adjust your own verbiage and actions first, and your team will naturally follow your lead. Therefore, in order to embed your team name into the culture of your business, it is up to you to first change your language when referring to your team. You must talk about your team name from the standpoint of a collective identity – on a consistent basis. If you want the team to engage and recognize that this identity is about the common good of the business, you must make an effort to speak about it.

Begin this adjustment by taking a step back and looking at how you typically refer to the business from the 10,000-foot view. Do you see yourself frequently using words and phrases like, "I think we should do this," "This is what I think is best for us," and "You need to do this"? If you do, make the focused effort to change your verbiage to phrases like (using your own team identity), "What would be the best thing for Tiger?" "What does Tiger need from us in this situation?" "How can we best serve and protect Tiger?"

When you as the leader speak this way, you are taking yourself out of the equation and putting the team's attention wholly on Tiger. You are also communicating in a way that will allow your team members to become more emotionally invested in the goals and future of the business.

Train yourself through consistent practice to maintain that level of awareness and discipline so that you do not revert back to the "I/me" style of communication. **The leader sets the pace for the speed of the race.** If you want your people to invest in the team identity, they need to consistently witness it in your words and actions.

**Live the Identity**

Once your team is following your lead, another way to incorporate your team identity into the culture of the business is through the use of objects and tokens. For instance, we make it a point to ensure that every member of Team Tiger receives a colorful stuffed tiger to invest them emotionally in the team identity, and it will be a constant reminder of why it's important to keep Tiger fed.

Your token could be a picture, a pen, a t-shirt – anything that weaves in the visual element of your team identity. I like to challenge our clients to be creative in the way they display their team name. One business we coach got together as a team and selected the identity, Rocky the Squirrel. And at each team meeting, there sits Rocky the stuffed, toy squirrel in the middle of the table, reminding each person who they're really working for and why it's important.

Have fun with your team name! Establish a monthly award based on customer kudos, sales statistics, or big ideas by team members. Create an award suggestion box where customers and team members can suggest nominees. Then at the end of the month, whichever nominee gets the most nods receives the company mascot and a gift, for instance, a stuffed tiger with a gift card tied around his furry neck.

Trophy recognition is an excellent day-to-day way of keeping your team identity at the forefront of your company culture.

Finally, connect all of this to the company goals to engage your team in the success of the business. If your goal is to take in one hundred new clients per year, make that Tiger's goal, and then celebrate as a team when it comes to fruition. The message you are communicating: if we all take care of Tiger and operate with the highest level of productivity and a positive mindset, that means we are giving back to Tiger and we will all be able to celebrate Tiger's success together!

**Empowerment Through Development**

The willingness to help your employees improve in their jobs, while making the effort to assess their personality styles, improve team communication, and help each person align with the goals of the business, is a stark contrast to leadership styles of business days past. Back then the boss was the boss, and he felt it was his duty to belittle people for what he perceived as "failing" in their job – whether he had provided them with development tools or not. Rather than making the effort to get to know his people and help them connect to the core values and mission of the company, typically high "D" personality bosses would issue the same workplace memo every day: "It's my way or the highway!"

That type of dictatorial leadership style tends not to work well in today's business environment. Employees today seek an emotional connection with how they fit in as individuals to the company mission, vision and culture. They want to know how they can personally contribute to the success of the business. Empowerment-based leadership has replaced intimidation-based leadership.

In business, we need to understand that today, employees are looking for greater meaning and stronger connections in their work. This does not mean, however, that we allow ourselves to go overboard, eliminating the necessary boundaries between manager and employees. We must always focus on what the business needs while finding a balance that allows employees to emotionally invest in the mission of the business. You can still be friendly, but always within the boundaries of solid business practices. Business is business and personal is personal.

We are now seeing the payoff of empowering our people through constant development, in all industries and all-sized businesses around the world. I am personally very excited by where business is headed. We have more power and resources at our fingertips than ever before to create a skilled, multi-talented, motivated team and truly drive our businesses to the Next Level of success. By gaining clarity and creating a solid plan of action in the Team Growth and Development facet of your Snapshot Business Plan, you are leveraging yourself and giving your business a strong infrastructure for growth. The sky's the limit!

### Goal Setting for the Team Growth and Development Facet of Your Business

This chapter has provided a process by which you can evaluate how well your team is meeting the needs of your business and then lay out action steps you can take to determine whether hiring, firing, or developing is what the business needs to move forward. Based on what you have learned, let's set goals for this facet of your Snapshot Business Plan.

### Consider these questions when setting goals for this facet of your business:

- Who are the people on your team?
- What skill sets do they have that are bringing great value to your business?
- Do you have good communication with them?

- Are they involved with your larger business goals?

- What development plans would best serve each team member?

- What kind of team members will help move your business forward this year?

- Do they have to be full-time? Could they be part-time? Could they be virtual or a contractor?

- Take the time to analyze your team growth and development. What is working and what is not working?

# CHAPTER NINE

# Sales Systems

*"I have never worked a day in my life without selling.
If I believe in something, I sell it, and I sell it hard."*

ESTÉE LAUDER

Nothing happens in business unless a sale is made. Yet some people in business get so mentally hung up on the word "sales" (gasp!) that the entire revenue-producing ability of their business is affected. It's up to you to make a shift in your thinking and understand that without sales, you do not have a business. If you do not create the opportunity to serve clients, then you are building a company with no foundation.

Perhaps as a result of the unspoken stigma, sales is one of the most commonly under-analyzed areas of business that I have seen in companies of all sizes. A successful sales facet requires purposefully and thoroughly looking at your sales system and understanding the best ways to manage all your activities associated with sales. Stop, look, and review what has worked for you (e.g., increased revenue) and what has not. Break it down even further by evaluating what you did to make those sales. What specific steps did you take that worked, and how can you duplicate that success over and over again? An organized, step-by-step method is needed in order to duplicate any kind of positive result in business. Let's look at what it takes to create a Sales facet that financially supports activity in the rest of your business.

**Levels of Contact**

When you start to identify your sales system, you must be aware of all the activities that surround each sale. Much of those activities will come directly out of your marketing facet, as dollars and effort. When it comes to bringing the leads into your business that are later converted into sales, the Marketing and Sales facets overlap. For instance, at events like business conferences and networking events, you invest marketing dollars to create presence with banners, business cards, and other promotional materials. Then, ideally as a result of that promotion, you attract leads that you funnel through your sales system and convert into revenue-producing clients. This is why it's so important to track marketing dollars and effort. When you do turn leads into clients, you can see the steps you took to make it happen and can then duplicate those steps over and over. Track what is feeding your sales funnel by getting clear on levels of contact.

Let's apply this information to networking events that I regularly attend. From the standpoint of my sales system, the first step is making the decision to attend the event. I ask myself questions like: Is my target audience there? Is the expected ROI (whether short- or long-term) worth the investment of my time and money? What will I need to do to prepare for the event (print business cards and other marketing materials, pay a membership or event fee, etc.)? It's important to be realistic about the opportunity at hand before you invest your time and marketing dollars in a sales opportunity.

Next, after deciding to attend the event, I perform my due diligence on the networking group and other attendees. Every group has a different dynamic and set of objectives. With some, the focus is on client referrals. Other groups encourage relationship building among members. Some organizations focus directly on sales and marketing. Regardless of the group dynamic, however, the basic tenets of sales apply – listen more than you speak, get to know the people around you, and understand what people need or what problem they are looking to solve. Can you solve their problem or refer them to someone else who can? Then, have an established plan for follow-up after the event.

Depending on the type and size of your business, leads come into your sales funnel through many different avenues. Check which ones pertain to your business:

- Live events (conducted by you)
- Live events that you attend (such as seminars, conferences, etc.)
- Your website
- Referrals (from past clients, business associates)
- Direct-mail marketing
- Email marketing
- Webinars
- Social media (Facebook, LinkedIn, Instagram, Twitter, Google Plus, etc.)

# Sales Funnel

### Example for a Real Estate Company

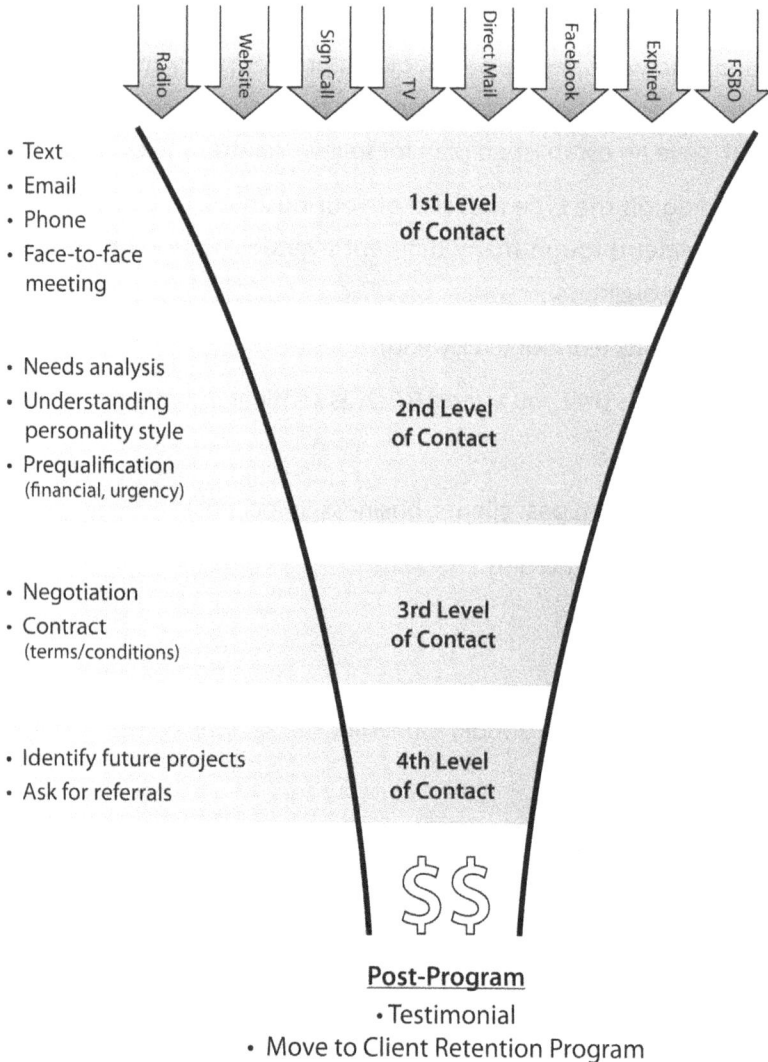

Radio · Website · Sign Call · TV · Direct Mail · Facebook · Expired · FSBO

- Text
- Email
- Phone
- Face-to-face meeting

**1st Level of Contact**

- Needs analysis
- Understanding personality style
- Prequalification (financial, urgency)

**2nd Level of Contact**

- Negotiation
- Contract (terms/conditions)

**3rd Level of Contact**

- Identify future projects
- Ask for referrals

**4th Level of Contact**

$$

### Post-Program

- Testimonial
- Move to Client Retention Program

Illustration 9.1

Track and measure the success of each item on the list. Look at metrics like geographical area, number of pieces sent, number of calls received, and conversion rate.

The level of contact you establish with each prospect will vary based on the scenario in which you and your prospect first connect. For example, how you follow up with an email lead may differ in procedure from how you follow up with leads you obtained from a networking event. It's important to identify the different avenues of contact in your sales system ahead of time and have a clear, consistent procedure in place for converting each one from lead to prospect to client. Tracking your conversion rate is essential to determine where you or your salespeople need skills improvement. This is where sales training can be a valuable addition to your Snapshot Business Plan for the year.

Here are the key steps in sales follow through:

1. Research the opportunity at hand, in this case a networking event. Evaluate whether the expected return justifies the investment of your time and marketing dollars.

2. Prepare yourself by understanding the "rules" of each level (e.g., the networking group's allowed promotion techniques, style of ad copy a newspaper typically runs, etc.).

3. Plan your follow-up based on your initial level of contact, whether through an email drip campaign, a personalized email, a phone call, or a face-to-face meeting.

## Qualifying Prospects

Have you heard the one about the real estate agent who was just so eager to make a sale – any sale – that she chose not to prequalify her prospects? She then spent hours and days driving these prospects around neighborhoods, here and there, burning gas and time, showing them dozens of properties. She was a tour guide not getting paid for the tour! A potential buyer would call and state with urgency, "I've got to see this house this afternoon!" Our friendly tour guide, always eager to get a sale, would hop into her car and burn rubber to reach the eager buyer as quickly as possible. She was driven entirely by a mindset of lack of revenue. Her mantra was, "If I do something, anything, I'll get some money." Her mission was based on a hope and a prayer. Then, after investing all that time and effort, when it came time to run the buyer's numbers, she found out that the person wasn't even close to being financially qualified to purchase a house.

A sale, like life, is not a perfect science. If every single lead that came into our business was magically converted into a contract, well, then every business out there would be a financial success story! The reality is that not every customer is meant to do business with every company. The process of sifting through leads and finding the right customers for your business is like dating. You go on a first date, ask questions to help determine whether this person might be a match for what you're looking for, listen to their answers, and then decide if you want to pursue the relationship.

Also similar to dating, no matter how long you've been at it, there is always something new to learn about qualifying prospects in sales. Regardless of how long you have worked in sales, you must always work to refine your selling skills, which are really listening skills. If you listen skillfully, you can identify and then meet the needs of your client prospect; then, you are really providing a service. The sales prequalification process ensures that you honor your business by being clear on your process of matching your products and services to the clients who need them.

**Sales Pre-qualification:**

1. Ask targeted questions.
2. Listen carefully to the answers.
3. Determine if and how you can provide the best product or service.
4. Ask for the sale.

Final step: Once you have the contract, then deliver the product or service.

This is where the sales prequalifying procedure intersects with your levels of contact system. After you have prequalified a lead as a potential client, the next step is to categorize them so you can determine the next level of contact in following up with them. I recommend "A, B, and C" categories customized for your business. For instance:

A:  The prospect definitely needs your product/service in the next 30 days.

B:  The prospect is very interested and will likely take action in the next 90 days.

C:  This person is either exhibiting only a small amount of interest in your product/service or won't be in a position financially to take advantage of your product or service for at least 90 days up to a one-year period.

While anyone past this period can be added to your database to receive your generic marketing (such as a newsletter), there are some leads that won't make your list at all; you just don't feel they'll ever be a good fit for your business. Don't clutter your database by adding them. It's not worth it. Unless, of course, they have a large sphere and you believe there is a possibility they could be a good referral source for you.

Once you categorize the prospect, it is now your job to keep asking questions and gathering information until you either convert them from prospect to client or determine that the relationship is not a good fit and remove them from your sales funnel.

For example, imagine you are a salesperson at a designer purse store on Rodeo Drive in Beverly Hills. A woman enters the store carrying an old version of one of the bags you sell. You can immediately categorize her as an A or B, simply because the evidence shows she is already a fan of your product. If you take the time to ask questions, find out this woman's needs, and build a relationship, there's a good chance that at some point she will buy from you.

Whenever prequalifying prospects, it's key to make objective decisions based on the evidence at hand, not what you hope and wish to be true. Look at the client's budget, identify where they are in the purchasing process, and determine realistically if there is a way you can work with this client. Your time is valuable in sales – far too valuable to waste it trying fruitlessly to turn a C client into an A client. If you engage in practices like this, you will likely invest your valuable time and money going in circles and fail to honor your business in the process.

Depending on the situation, it may be necessary to tell the person, "I don't think my products/services are a fit for you at this point in time." It's better for you and the other person to be honest now. You owe this to your business, and frankly, you owe it to the prospect too.

To deliver an even greater level of insight as to what it takes to develop and maintain a finely-tuned sales system that delivers results, I spoke with a true expert on the subject. Alice Heiman has been training sales teams to succeed for many years.

*"Let's start by discussing your sales funnel, also commonly called your sales pipeline or opportunities manager – all the same thing. Picture a funnel – large at the top, small at the bottom. A sales funnel is the place, whether a computerized program or a basic spreadsheet, where you organize your sales objectives. A sales objective is a clearly-stated opportunity to sell to a prospect that you met out in your prospecting travels. For instance, you're out there networking, talking to lots and lots of people, and suddenly someone raises their hand and says, "Yes, I am interested in your services." You immediately drop that person into the top of your funnel and identify a sales objective like, "Sell John Smith X dollars of Y service by Z date." Then, enter details like John's contact information, the date the objective was created, the product or service they've expressed interest in, when they want to buy, etc. Enter this information immediately, so you don't forget and*

*allow a potential customer to get lost in the daily shuffle of doing business.*

*Next, you start moving John Smith down through your sales funnel by qualifying him as a sales prospect.*

**Qualifying Step 1:** *Do your homework. What can you find out ahead of time about a prospect before you meet with them? This is very easy to do with the Internet. You can check their website, their social media sites, read Google alerts about them, news articles, their blog, and more. Know as much about the prospect and their business ahead of time as possible.*

**Qualifying Step 2:** *Ask good questions and then be quiet and listen to the answers. Most people rush into selling before they even know if the prospect needs or wants their services. My dad's business partner once put it this way: 'Hey Mr. Customer, I have a solution to a problem which neither you nor I completely understand – wanna buy it?' I always say sales equals problem solving and you can't solve a problem that you don't understand. Good questions to ask include: How do they already do what you're offering to do for them in a different way? Is that working for them? What would they like to be able to do that they can't do now? Why are they looking for a solution at this time? What has changed? These questions help them understand their own problem while helping you to understand so you can solve it.*

**Qualifying Step 3:** *Dig even deeper. Once you have determined there is a need (i.e., a problem you can solve), you need to qualify them further, thus dropping them even deeper into your sales funnel. The prospect may have a need; however, their budget or timeline may disqualify them at this particular time. In addition to inquiring about their timeline and budget, ask questions like: 'How will you make this decision? Who else besides yourself will be involved in the decision-making process? Would a payment plan help my services fit your budget better? What other solutions have you considered similar to mine (competitors)?'*

*These three steps are essential in preventing your prospects from stalling at the close. You'll be able to identify a stalled prospect when you're trying to get them to sign on the dotted line and they say things like, 'I need some more time to think about it.' This generally indicates that they either don't have the money, something about the solution is not a good fit for them, or it's simply not the right time for them.*

*You cannot rush the qualifying process. It is what it is. Qualify all your prospects by following these three steps and that will help your sales process move along faster without making the prospects feel rushed.*

*Now, back to your sales funnel, where you have just successfully qualified a prospect. The next step is to verify that we still have a solid sales objective moving forward, that the individual is still on board. Once you've done that and all lights are green, the prospect drops to the very bottom part of your funnel – the close. This is when they sign on the dotted line, write you a check, leave your sales funnel, and take their place on your production line.*

*The most important thing about a sales funnel is keeping the top very full of prospects at all times. You will determine, through your sales tracking, how many prospects at the top of the funnel turn into closed deals at the bottom. It may be ten at the top for every two that make it down to the bottom. Some will fall out of your funnel as the qualification and verification processes go on, either due to price, timeline, or choice of another vendor. Some you may personally choose not to do business with. The bottom line is to continue moving each prospect through your sales funnel, following all the steps, until you either lose the deal or close the deal."*

In business, it is one of your ongoing jobs to constantly fine-tune your sales skills, your prospect-qualifying process, your sales funnel, and your overall sales process. Even if you were the most amazing salesperson on the planet five years ago, you must always be seeking out new opportunities to listen to prospects better and serve clients better. When writing your goals for this facet, think about constant improvements to your sales skills and your system.

You've already invested a lot of money, through marketing, to generate the leads. It's vital to understand how well you're converting those leads, what you can do to improve, so that a greater percentage make it to the end of your funnel.

**Consider these questions when setting goals for the sales facet of your business:**

- What sales processes are currently working for you?
- Who is responsible for them?
- Are you getting the desired results?
- Do you have powerful tracking processes that allow you to determine if your sales system is working?
- What other ideas would you like to implement in your business?

CHAPTER TEN

# Customer Retention

"Customer satisfaction is worthless.
Customer loyalty is priceless."

JEFFREY GITOMER

I have a favorite clothing store where I am a very frequent shopper – so frequent that the salespeople call me at home when they're having a special, when a new item comes in that matches my preferences, or even if it's been awhile and they're checking to see if I have needs. I love the products they sell, I have great relationships with the staff, and I feel good just walking in the door. I am a regular customer, and this store has mastered the art of retaining me.

There is a famous sales tenet that it's easier to retain a customer than acquire a new one. But how do you stay in contact with the people who have used your products/services before to ensure that they buy again? The key to finding success in the Customer Retention facet of your business is staying in regular contact with your customers. As the old adage says, "Out of sight, out of mind." The goals you set in this area will be based on your system for remaining consistently connected to your customers, both past and present.

How do you keep in touch?

- Email newsletter
- Personal emails
- Birthday/holiday greeting cards
- Seasonal messages
- Sending gifts/promotional items
- Phone calls
- Direct mail
- Social media
- In-person meetings (coffee, lunch, dinner)

Once someone has done business with you, don't assume they will automatically come back and do business with you again. Doing business with past or existing customers is a very powerful way of purposefully increasing revenue. You have, after all, already made the effort to prequalify them as clients, move them through your sales funnel, provide a quality product or service that they need, and then ensure they're satisfied with the outcome. This is far too valuable an investment to simply walk away from. Your past and existing customers are also referral sources for you. When people like what it is that you're selling, they will keep buying from you and also tell their friends.

How do you retain and keep those customers even if they're not currently doing business with you? You have the power to do this by creating a systematic approach for staying in touch with those individuals. Develop a well-organized customer database that makes it easy, convenient, and even automated for you to connect and communicate with your contacts without any large lapses of time in between touches (thus allowing them to forget about you).

The time to create your customer retention program is when you're doing your business planning for the upcoming year. Review your budget to determine what the business can afford and then look at your client database. When determining the best way of touching each client, there are a few things to consider:

- Their preferred method of communication

- How often they refer new clients to you

- The amount and frequency of their investment in your product/service

Similar to how you categorized prospects during the lead-prequalification process, group clients by how you plan to stay in touch with them. For instance, the way you touch clients in your "platinum" group will be different than the way you connect with your "gold" clients (who are one level down from your platinum). How you group clients in your database, how you name those groups, by what means, and how often you contact them is a judgment call on your part. We believe that monthly is a minimum for being in front of your database, be it by e-newsletter, postcard, or any other method of communication. Remember, you're reaching out to people who already know you, with a twofold purpose: first, to remind them you're still in the business; and second, to let them know you care about them. This can be achieved in a variety of ways.

**Priority of Effective Communication Avenues for Powerful Results:**

1. The most powerful place is face to face, individually.

   To boost referrals, would it make sense to schedule at least one weekly coffee meeting with one of your best referring sources?

2. Meeting face to face when in a group.

   If your clients and customers are local, and a manageable number, would a live client-appreciation event be a possibility?

If you have a storefront, what about hosting an event in your own space?

3. Engaging in a two-way conversation on the telephone.

How often are you getting on the phone with past clients and customers? Again, the size and scope of your business will dictate, to a degree, whether this is practical. With your key clients, do you call to wish them a happy birthday or check in to see what has changed since last you spoke?

4. Hearing your voice on a voicemail message.

There is true value and appreciation when past clients are able to simply hear your voice. They feel connected. Don't let the fear that you don't have time for a lengthy conversation prevent you from calling. There are even services available where you can pre-record a message, or have your call go directly into the recipient's voice mail, saving time but still accomplishing the goal of having an emotional connection.

5. Receiving a handwritten note.

Knowing that someone has taken the time to put the effort into a personalized, handwritten message leaves the recipient feeling special and important – and they are.

6. Receiving a private text message.

The recipient knows that you are reaching out to just them right now, and it sends a message that they are the most important person to you in this moment.

7. Receiving a personal email.

Similar to a text message in its value, while perhaps not as immediate, this is a great way to put the focus on them. Consider what the preferred method of communication is for the individual.

8.  Receiving a group email.

    Because this is a hand-selected group of people, this indicates they've been selected for a reason, not randomly contacted. Again, you're creating a feeling of being valued.

9.  Receiving a personalized marketing piece in the mail.

    You could easily send only marketing that's not addressed to any specific person. However, by taking the time to address it specifically to this one person (think mail merge on a letter to use their first name), you demonstrate appreciation by taking the extra step.

10. Receiving a marketing email.

    This type of communication can be effective when needing to communicate with a large group of people and is most effective when well written and including some sort of call to action.

Think about the image advertising pros. If I mention the word "soda," what pops into your mind? Most likely it's Coke® or Pepsi®, as a result of their high brand visibility. Your business doesn't have to be at that level to replicate that success either! I know a mortgage lender who sends out extremely professional, vibrant newsletters each quarter, often with recipe cards enclosed. Who do you think her customers think of when they're cooking up those recipes in the kitchen? And when someone that customer knows is looking for a referral to a mortgage lender, whose name do you think comes to mind? She makes the effort to consistently stay in front of her customers, and therefore she remains at the forefront of their minds, even in between those touches. You always want to be top of mind with people who have done business with you. The goal is to remain visible to your customers at all times. Whether on social media or in a face-to-face meeting, you have to be in front of people so they will buy from you.

Going back to our key Snapshot Business Planning questions using this facet as an example:

- *What's working?* John Brown consistently contracts me; how can I thank him? Do I send a gift directly to him or make a donation to a charity in his name?

- *What's not working?* I have all these people who have done business with me, but I don't have a clear system for staying connected with them.

- *What goals can I set?* I see I have the budget and time to send something to my past and present clients (holiday cards, birthday cards, etc.).

**Consider these questions when setting goals for this facet of your business:**

- What are the top three reasons customers keep coming back?

- What are the steps in establishing an effective customer retention campaign?

- What new ideas would you like to incorporate into your business?

# CHAPTER ELEVEN

# Technology and Equipment

"Technology is best when it brings people together."

MATT MULLENWEG

Is your technology and equipment making you as efficient as possible? This facet of your business goes well beyond having the latest electronic gadgets and a printer that doesn't jam. Your technology and equipment should support the productivity and profitability of your business. Paying attention to this area is very important; it allows you to assess what you need to best serve your business and your goals. Let's take a tour of your office and see what's working, what's not, and what goals need to be set.

## Hardware

All the physical equipment in your office, including printers, phone headsets, your computer, shredder, and more, falls under the hardware heading. How is each item working for you? Is any of your hardware outdated and restricting the speed and efficiency (and thus productivity and profitability) of your daily activities? For instance, if your printer is slow as molasses, it may be time to make a purchase. Once you make that decision, you must then look at your financials and determine the cost of the purchase and the best time to make it (e.g., second quarter of the year versus fourth).

Here's an example of how bad hardware had a negative impact on one company's bottom line. One of our coaching clients, a CEO, had no idea that the printer was always jamming, because his dutiful administrative assistant thought she was protecting him by avoiding a costly new purchase. What she didn't see, however, was the big picture – the 10,000-foot view. The printer was jamming two to three times per week, and she and her co-workers were weighed down by constant frustration and lost productivity as a result. The CEO remained blissfully unaware of this technological turmoil in his office, until we sat down to do his Snapshot Business Planning and arrived at this facet. When I posed the question, "What's not working?" the assistant and several others were quick to chime in, "The printer!" Once the issue was on the table, we determined that the cost of a new printer, in the long run, was substantially lower than the cost of the lost productivity caused by the broken printer.

This is a great example of how this type of business planning allows both you and your team to zoom out from the day-to-day details and see the big picture. When you involve your team members in the business-planning process, they become invested in finding solutions for what is not working in the business. They also have a stronger, clearer understanding of the value of each goal that is set. This greater level of meaning and motivation drives them to deliver at a higher level when it comes time to work toward those goals. When people understand the "why" they become more invested in the "what."

Sometimes it's the hardware you don't have that's getting in the way of your growth. Revisit the other seven facets. Take marketing, for example. If blogging to increase your Search Engine Optimization is part of next year's plan, maybe video blogging would take it to the next level. Do you have the hardware you want to create quality videos? What would the cost be? When does it make sense to incorporate this into the budget?

Again, this is an opportunity to engage the team. What missing hardware could be key in leveraging them to their desired level of success? Would a second monitor allow them to cross-check data without having to toggle between applications? Remember, the request for an expenditure needs to be accompanied by a thoughtful and sensible explanation of the tangible, as well as the intangible, benefits. Involving your team will reinforce the lesson of ROI and the importance of protecting "Tiger."

A note of caution with hardware: sometimes we'll sacrifice a little functionality to save a buck. This can be a huge detriment down the road. For those who can remember, in 1981 a computer was released with 640 kilobytes of storage, and no one could fathom how that could get used up. One of our clients filled up a one-terrabyte (there are a billion kilobytes in a terrabyte) external hard drive just with recreational digital photos she'd taken! If given the choice to make a significant upgrade for a modest price increase, seriously consider the opportunity.

## Software

Continuing our tour of your office, we arrive at the technological brains that drive productivity and profit in this facet – your software. How are the programs and applications that you invest in driving all areas of your business? The core pieces of technology critical to any business are contact management and a backup system in case your systems go down. But beyond those pieces, which technology is needed to support the needs of your business?

For example, perhaps you have an antiquated sales system that has people tracking leads through Excel spreadsheets. This might have worked in the past, but wouldn't an upgrade to a comprehensive client-relationship management (CRM) software make it more efficient for your salespeople, their supervisors, and you to track movement on sales leads in real time? Inefficient tracking of sales leads doesn't give you the information needed to measure the effectiveness of your salespeople and your marketing.

After finally putting software in place, one of our clients discovered that one of his salespeople was a rock star at closing leads; another, not so much. He determined that the non-rock star needed more training on sales scripts, listening skills, and the ability to ask for a sale. By upgrading the sales software, he had more knowledge on each individual's productivity and was able to step in with targeted training to increase productivity.

Next, what technology systems do you have in place that connect and streamline multiple facets? The rule with software is to try to invest in a few highly-efficient, easy-to-use programs that benefit all areas of your business (versus using a different application for each task within the business).

Looking at your software, are there any upgrades needed? Are there more recent versions of your existing programs that could better serve your business? Have you budgeted for upgrades and updates at the time of your purchase? How will you train your people on new technology – through online tutorials or will it have to be via hands-on training, investments that cross over to your team growth and development facet?

Consider the crossovers into other facets of your business as well. Perhaps upgrading your bookkeeping software may provide you with the additional data needed to strengthen your financial facet. Or maybe a new sales program would work better with your sales funnel. Is there a training application that could help your people reach goals set in the team growth and development area? Go through each area of your business and identify which software is in place to increase productivity and profitability. Then do some research, and see what else is on the market that could do the job even better. One of the key components of Snapshot Business Planning is constant, thorough evaluation of what's working and what can be improved upon.

Some hardware needs have become software possibilities – is it time to replace your onsite server with a cloud-based solution, for example? Weigh the "anytime, anywhere" convenience against the risk of having no connectivity (while rare, it's still possible to find ourselves without access to the Internet from time to time).

## Equipment Inventory

Many businesses don't keep an inventory of what they have purchased. How can you plan for investing in new equipment when you don't know what you have already and when it's likely to need to be replaced from wear? Are you just waiting for it to break, putting you in an emergency situation where you need to order it fast off the shelf, without the benefit of price shopping first? Keeping an accurate, up-to-date inventory at all times will help you plan and prepare for upcoming investments (thus protecting you from hurting your financials due to emergency purchases), allowing you to build them into your budget. By doing this, for instance, you might realize that your laptop is four years old, and you will need to plan ahead to invest in a new one next quarter. The other benefit of maintaining an inventory list is in the event of an unforeseen natural disaster. Your insurance provider likely has an existing tool you can use to catalog what you have and therefore what would need to be replaced in an emergency.

## Tech Support

With all technology, it's key to have a support structure in place for when programs need upgrades or, in the case of equipment, when things break down. Does technical support come with purchase, or will you need to invest in a technical repairperson? Will that person be on retainer or charge by the hour? How quick is their response time? These are all questions that you need to ask when setting up your technology and equipment in a way that serves the needs of your business.

Finally, when your technology no longer serves the needs of your business, I encourage you to consider recycling it. Investigate local nonprofit entities that would benefit from a partnership with your business. Think about how many people – schools, adult learning centers, shelters, churches, non-profits, etc. – could benefit from your old computers! Just because the hard drive isn't fast enough to do desktop publishing (if that's what your business requires), doesn't mean it's officially a useless piece of junk. Remember the old adage: "One person's trash is another person's treasure." There may also be a tax benefit in the donation. Be sure to consult your tax advisor on what your options are.

**Consider these questions when setting goals for this facet of your business:**

- Take an inventory of all the hardware that you have. Does anything need to be repaired, replaced, or added?

- Take the time to analyze your hardware and software. What is working and what is not working?

- What quarter of the year are the repairs or purchases best incurred?

- What new software programs do you need to upgrade or purchase next year?

- Is there anyone on your team, including yourself, who needs training in the software so that both the software and the person can truly support your business goals?

# CHAPTER TWELVE

# Office

"*We are what we see. We are products of our surroundings.*"

AMBER VALLETTA

How do you feel when you walk into your office – happy and productive or anxious because of the clutter and disorganization? When you think of challenges related to your physical office space, do words like organization or clutter come to mind? While those are key things to look at, the Office facet of your Snapshot Business Plan is about more than Feng Shui and file cabinets.

Your office is your environment for productivity and profitability. From your organizational tools to technology to the decorations on the wall, the space you create to do your work in is very much connected to the work you do in the other facets of your business. What feels and works best for you?

Let's start breaking down this facet of your business plan by asking the Snapshot Business Planning questions you're likely very familiar with by this point in the book: What's working and what's not working in your office environment? What goals need to be set for improvement?

Here is a step-by-step method to help you determine the answers to these questions and the goals you need to set in the Office facet.

### 1. Take a Tour of Your Space

Make a list of everything in your office, from physical location down to each file cabinet and wall hanging. Evaluate how well each item supports your feeling of productivity in your office. In the case of the wall hangings, other items that decorate your space and even the color scheme, assess how your décor reflects the core values and unique identity of your business. Is your office visually motivating? Does it make you feel powerful? Never underestimate the psychology of a well-organized, nicely designed office.

How do you track your goals visually? One often-overlooked and exceptionally valuable visual support is goal tracking. In your financial facet, you set specific targets. How do you stay visually aware of progress? You may choose to put up a production thermometer that gets colored in as each new client, unit sale, or other method of measure is accomplished. For your team, you might have a white board in a common area showing where each salesperson is in relation to their goals for the month and the year. Note that administrative team members appreciate being able to participate in the tracking toward the team's end goal as well.

Looking at your list as a whole, how well does your office in its current form support you in your work every day? What works on the list? What doesn't and therefore needs to be changed?

### 2. Evaluate the Size and Location

How is the current location and size of your space working for the needs of your business? How is it working against you? Is the time right to expand the space or even purchase a building? If you owned, could you sublease some of the space and supplement your investment with some income? If you currently own your space (whether an entire building or space in one), is it time to sell or renew your lease? Do you have a storefront and are you responsible for building upkeep as well? How does this arrangement serve the growth of your business? Is continuing on with this lease the best decision you can make? Review the dynamics of what the business needs and plan for the best decision that you can make this year.

When it comes to the specific decision of whether to negotiate, renew, or cancel your lease, consider what your office is costing you. This goes beyond the rent or the lease. The total cost of your office, as pertaining to the financial facet of your Snapshot Business Plan, encompasses utilities, staffing, your commute, parking fees, supplies, and everything else needed to maintain the space. Ask yourself:

- Are the terms of your lease (like length, for example) conducive to your present needs?

- Do you really need an office outside your home (i.e., does the business need it)?

- Do you now need an even larger office?

- What is your ROI of having an outside office?

- Would a collaborative space be a sufficient option to meet your needs?

Remember, with Snapshot Business Planning, each facet is connected to the others and flows together into an interconnected picture of what your business needs to reach the Next Level. In this case, the decisions you make in your office facet directly connect with your goals in the marketing and financial facets. And as with the other facets, it's important to evaluate the answers to all the questions above on a regular basis to ensure that your office space is supporting the needs of your business.

**Case Study #1:** _____

> *Our real estate client had a five-year lease that was up for renewal, but to her surprise, the landlord refused any type of negotiation. So, she met with her financial advisor and her commercial broker, looked at other properties, and discovered that she was in a position to purchase a building of her own. Over time, ownership had become a better decision for the business. For this client, an inflexible landlord became a blessing in disguise for the business, forcing her to explore her options, and take the leap to building ownership!*

**Case Study #2:** _____

> *An independent contractor had also been leasing space in a building but now another landlord was wooing them. The contractor asked for my help in deciding which option was the better deal. I posed these questions: Do you like the environment, the neighborhood, and the parking situation? What about the upkeep arrangement? Do you like the people (other tenants) you're surrounded by? Do you like your current landlord? Is the equipment always working? In this case, with her answer being a resounding "yes" to each of these questions, it was better for this client's business to stay put. It's not always about every dollar. When making decisions like these, it's important to look at the big picture, the view from 10,000 feet, and carefully weigh all the pros and cons.*

### 3. Organizational Efficiency

Next, let's look at the working space within your office. Is everything, from furniture to technology, arranged in an efficient manner? How well does it support your productivity? For example, do you have to constantly get up and run across the room every time you need to get something off the printer? What action steps can you take to make yourself and your space as efficient as possible? Do you need to purchase any new technology, furniture, or other supplies to improve the efficiency of your workspace?

## 4. Time to Purge

Okay, let's move on to the issue of all that clutter getting in the way of your productivity. People have a tendency to keep clutter because they don't have a plan of how to sort it, process it, and then decide what to do about it.

**Key Questions to Ask:**

1.  Where are you saving your archived files?

2.  Do you have paper files? If so, can they be scanned and saved electronically to free up physical office space?

3.  Can you put your physical files into storage?

4.  Have you identified how long you need to keep different types of legal and official records and files? Have you put them on recurring reminders to reduce that paper on the approved timetable?

5.  What else can you do to streamline how you collect and store papers and files?

As a frequent attendee of seminars and conferences, and a rapid handwritten note-taker, it would be very easy for me to amass a veritable mountain of paperwork in my office. One solution is to scan your notes, save them on your computer and then toss them. Which of your habits can you address with a plan of action for preventing clutter before it occurs?

To battle clutter, you must have a clearly designed plan in place. My personal favorite way of clearing clutter is what I call the laundry basket exercise.

**Laundry Basket Exercise**

1. Gather all papers off your desk, chair, briefcase, or wherever else you have them stashed away and get a laundry basket. (A box or any other large container will work just as well.) Put everything into the laundry basket without sneaking a peek at anything. Set aside a specific amount of time to address each item in the basket.

2. Apply the One-Touch Paper Method. The goal is to empty the basket. As you pick up each piece of paper, make a decision to place it on one of the following piles. The paper cannot leave your hand until you make the decision where it belongs – no shuffling! Do NOT take action on anything (such as make a call or type up an email). Move the paper to the appropriate pile/folder. I recommend that you create a pile or file folder for each of the following:

   a. **Read** – items that you want to browse or need to read.

   b. **Work In Progress (W.I.P.)** – items you have already worked on and require a response to or from someone.

   c. **To Do** – tasks that you personally need to do, such as call, email, etc.

   d. **Ditch** – items to get rid of now. Have a garbage can/recycle bin sitting next to you and be ruthless.

   e. **Delegate** – items for others. Attach a sticky note to the person you are delegating to or have a file with their name on it.

   f. **File** – items that simply need to be put away.

3. Go ahead and purge that Ditch pile. Then set aside all other file folders or piles except the one marked To Do. Separate the tasks from the To Do folder into Personal and Business and document them on your Personal To-Do List or Business To-Do List.

4.  Next, go to the Delegate stack. What timelines are you going to set for the person to complete the task? How will you follow up to keep that person accountable to completion? Have a clear end date and process for each, and then assign them out.

5.  For the Work In Progress pile, if you're waiting on someone else, make sure that a follow-up action has been scheduled on your calendar. If you're the hold up, turn to your calendar right now and allocate time for completing whatever your next step is.

6.  With your Read pile, do you have time on a monthly basis set aside to do just that? If you value it, schedule it. If you don't, then ditch it!

7.  Be committed to your plan and execute. Sometimes we call this process "Ready, Aim Fire!" Don't get stuck on Aim, Aim, and Aim. Make sure that you Fire ~ Execute ~ Make it Happen!

**Goal Setting for the Office Facet of your Business**

When setting goals for this and all facets, remember to write each one as a **SMART** goal – that is **S**pecific, **M**easurable, **A**ttainable, **R**ealistic, and **T**ime-limited. What are the specific action steps needed to accomplish the goal? What is the date you'd like to achieve the goal by? Who can help you achieve this goal?

**Also consider:**

•   Do you have enough space?

•   Do you need to renegotiate your lease?

•   Is it a great time to purchase?

•   Do you need to clear out some clutter?

•   Do you need to make purchases for your office?

- Take the time to analyze your office. What is working and what is not working?

One final consideration: if you have a team, they are impacted by their surroundings as well, and their opinions about the space are important to consider. What suggestions do they have for changes or improvements? In some cases, it might even be useful to bring in a spatial planner or interior design consultant. A fresh set of eyes can bring a different and valuable perspective.

# CHAPTER THIRTEEN

# Celebration

Why is Celebration important? We have a tendency to do a lot of celebration for others – birthdays, promotions, anniversaries, sports victories – but we overlook our own personal accomplishments in business (and in life). When we take the time to recognize that we've accomplished something – finished a project ahead of schedule, exceeded a sales goal, or discovered a way to save the company money – inside we experience a positive vibration that raises our confidence, establishes us at a higher level of productivity, and sets us up for additional successes.

The same holds true with our lives. Most of us realize that success in life only comes with the balance of success in our business and personal lives. In the constant chaos that is in today's world, we so seldom pause long enough to reflect on the small daily accomplishments that mean so much to our overall bigger picture of what we wish for our lives. Recognize what you've accomplished and find a way to celebrate.

Here's a personal daily habit that will help you celebrate the person you are becoming. Take five minutes at the end of each day and journal your accomplishments from the day. Challenge yourself to think not only in terms of your work tasks but in your life choices as well. Were you up and at the gym for 30 minutes to start your day energized? Did you schedule time to attend a social event with your significant other? Did your meal planning over the weekend result in a wonderful, home-cooked meal with your family? Celebrate those achievements.

Turning back to business, throughout your Snapshot Business Plan, you've set numerous goals within each of the facets. Each of these creates an opportunity for celebration. When it comes to the "smaller" achievements, it might be as simple as giving yourself permission to grab a specialty coffee, go for a walk on the beach, or even take a nap. More substantial goals may merit more substantial celebrations.

Make up a list of ways that you can celebrate, from those small celebrations that cost absolutely no money to more substantial celebrations, like taking a vacation or buying a new car. Come up with at least three possible ways that you would like to celebrate in the following categories:

- Absolutely free

_____

_____

_____

- Under $20

_____

_____

_____

- $20 to $50

_____

_____

_____

- $50 to $100

_____

_____

_____

- $100 to $200

_____

_____

_____

- Over $200

_____

_____

_____

Now shift to considering celebrations for your team. Again, both small and large achievements are motivating here. If the goal for the month is achieved, maybe you bring in lunch for the team. Perhaps a quarterly goal achievement results in the celebration of an evening out for bowling! One of our clients set a huge celebration goal with her team of going on a cruise if they hit their sales goals for the year. Note, I say with her team; she didn't choose the celebration on her own. She asked the team what would really motivate them and set a budget for what she was willing to spend. Talk about motivation! First, the team had fun participating in selecting the celebration. Second, they were highly motivated to achieve the goals.

Whether it's a decision made by you or a collective decision of the team, keep it simple. Repeat the process of identifying at least three possible ways that your team would like to celebrate in the following categories:

- Absolutely free

_____

_____

_____

- Under $20

_____

_____

_____

- $20 to $50

_____

_____

_____

- $50 to $100

_____

_____

_____

- $100 to $200

_____

_____

_____

- Over $200

_____

_____

_____

Celebration is important for you, as the leader, as well as for the team. Go back and review each of your Snapshot Business Planning facets, asking the following questions:

- What is the goal achievement you wish to focus on?
- What milestones along the way create opportunities to celebrate in smaller ways?
  - Sales targets
  - Project completion
  - Cost savings
- How will you celebrate?

# CHAPTER FOURTEEN

# Goal Summary and Action Steps

Congratulations, you made it through all 12 steps, including the eight key facets, to take your business to the Next Level! I promised you a painless, doable process, right? Take a moment to acknowledge yourself for investing this time to work on your business. You have taken a giant leap toward bringing your business to the Next Level. Now gather all of your notes and lists you've collected throughout this process. What you now have is your business plan for the next year. This is a truly powerful step!

This next step is a critical one. You have already set the goals that define how you'll move forward in each of the facets. Next, you will pull all of your goals together into just a couple of pages, making it easy for you to reference them and focus on them. Go back through your notes to the goals you wrote at the end of each chapter and move them onto a master list of goals for your business. This summary sheet is truly your Snapshot Business Plan for the upcoming year.

Now, choose six goals from this master list that would truly add value and cause the business to grow – what the business needs most urgently right now. The first goal of your top six will always be financial because you are in business to create revenue. As mentioned earlier, nothing happens in business unless a sale is made. Feeding your financial facet will in turn give you the flexibility to invest in all other areas of your business. Take a moment now to choose one financial facet goal and five additional goals from any facet. As you capture these goals, run them through the SMART formula, and make sure that each of your six lives up to its requirement – Specific, Measurable, Attainable, Realistic, and Time-limited.

Next, add the specific action steps you'll need to take to achieve each goal. For example, if your goal is to start using accounting software like QuickBooks, your steps will include purchasing the software, receiving training (or training the team member who will be responsible for using it), and setting up your bookkeeping systems.

In order to set your plan in motion, identify achieve-by dates for each of the action steps. Giving yourself deadlines for each goal and action step ensures that you'll follow through on each one. (Circle back and review the example detailed in the Products and Services facet.) I can't overstate the importance of getting specific on your action steps. What tools will you need to achieve the goal? Who will be involved in making it happen?

Remember to build accountability into the process too, whether this means progress reports to a business coach, mentor, colleague, or friend. So many of our clients tell us accountability was the key to their success. Having someone in your camp that you can look to for help, who asks the hard questions, and who can hold you to keeping your commitments can make all the difference in the world. Accountability gives you a structure to your life and work, and it not only helps you prioritize your actions but it is also a place to celebrate your successes. Finding a safe and insightful accountability partner, group, or coach is a simple but sure route to success. What form of accountability appeals to you? What step will you take now to get an accountability structure in place for yourself?

Finally, now is the time for you to have certainty and clarity about what you want to see happen in the next 12 months. When you spend time getting super clear about the goals in your Snapshot Business Plan, you will get excited about the next steps toward reaching those goals. If you don't get clear about what you are aiming at, you are much less likely to hit the mark.

Having these goal summary pages accessible to you throughout your days, weeks, and months ahead is key.

· · · · · · · · · · · · · · · · · · · · · · · · · · · · · · · · · · ·

*The proven process for achieving your goals is to focus on what you desire and set a purposeful plan to achieve them.*

· · · · · · · · · · · · · · · · · · · · · · · · · · · · · · · · · · ·

Consider posting your top six goals somewhere that you'll see them each day, and then schedule time to review your entire business plan summary, ideally once a month – at minimum once a quarter. As you achieve your top six goals, you can now move other items onto this short list from your Snapshot Business Plan summary pages.

Set time aside for a mid-year review to evaluate all the accomplishments you've made as well as items still residing on the list. As you review every facet of your business, consider the following:

1.  Acknowledge accomplishments. What have you achieved so far this year?

2.  Review and analyze. For the goals you set, do you need to make any adjustments?

3.  Clarify and commit. Has something new entered into your business considerations that wasn't important when you originally set these goals but is now a priority? If so, add it to the list.

You may choose to re-prioritize your goals within your top six, or add or change the top six to include new items. Some companies find they want to drill down to their top three – that's okay. What's most important is to be clear and focused on what the business needs.

The time you invest in business planning is always worth it, and now you just need to put the final touches on the plan and away we go. Here's to your successful year and making it great!

# Conclusion

"Believe in the desires you have for your business;
surround yourself with the right influencers
and success is yours!"
LINDA MCLEAN

Whether you are the owner or a leader within the organization, you are an influencer of the success and growth of the business. It is up to you to decide what you are going to do to take it to the Next Level. You must make the choice to visualize that level, put the right people in place within the organization, have a plan, set your goals, follow through, and be accountable for the results.

You have just gone through and evaluated every nook and cranny of your business to determine what you'd like to accomplish this year. You (and ideally your team) have invested quality time in working on your business while reading this book. You've created a blueprint for success. It is now your responsibility to set out, follow your plan, keep the right people engaged, maintain discipline, and stay dialed in from now through the end of the year when it's time to create next year's Snapshot Business Plan. When people fail to revisit this Snapshot Business Plan frequently, progress slows and sometimes stops altogether. Motivation will only carry you so far. With a positive mindset in place, constant accountability is the key to success in achieving the goals you have set throughout this book. Continuously apply everything you have learned, and your Next Level is there for the taking!

When you stay plugged into this process, you operate and vibrate at a higher level of productivity. It's like the hope and excitement you feel when you're getting ready to go on vacation. The possibilities of what may happen are endless. Maintaining this momentum, this excitement, is key in any business.

Final thoughts:

- Hold tight to the vision that you've cast.
- Put things into motion with purposeful planning.
- Be disciplined in your follow-through.
- Stay grounded in making smart decisions.
- Celebrate your accomplishments.

Remember, you don't know where you're going until you pick a destination. The possibilities for your business truly are infinite! Embrace every day and enjoy the journey of building your business.

# Are You Ready for Coaching?

So that's it... almost!

I've certainly tried to pack as much as possible into this book. Still, the information I've shared with you has, of necessity, been kept more on the "general" side of things. That is, most of it applies to most people and most businesses in most situations.

That's because any book that even tried to take into account every single variable that every single reader might run into, in both your business and private life, would be too unwieldy, too expensive, and still fall far short of its goal.

Nonetheless, we've gone into enough detail here that I believe most readers will be able to take this as a jumping-off point and then dig deeper into the specifics of their own situation – applying these strategies as they go.

And, of course, if you've followed along and completed the exercises, you likely now have a business plan in hand and are ready for the next step.

But we all have different strengths and weaknesses, and while some readers might breeze through this material in a short time, there are undoubtedly others who are still challenged by some of the steps we've covered.

And even if you DO have that business plan in hand and are ready for the next step, you might still need some additional guidance now or maybe further down the road.

If you're in either of those groups, take heart, because you're in good company.

It's the many tiny details that bring the "big picture" to life!

You see, no matter how long you've been doing what you do, it is often beneficial to have someone OUTSIDE your business look INTO your business. It's that old "forest for the trees" paradox:

The closer you are to something, the harder it is to really "see" it!

And the tighter your focus, the more difficult it can be to see how all the pieces fit together. It's like staring at a single jigsaw puzzle piece and never looking at the picture on the box.

That's where a good coach can make all the difference for you!

An experienced business coach, like those on our team here at McLean International, can drill down into those microscopic details of your business while maintaining that 10,000-foot view. (Using the jigsaw puzzle analogy again: Every tiny piece is critical to your success – but only as it fits into, and adds to, the overall big picture.)

In fact, coaches are the powerful "secret weapon" of some of the busiest, most successful entrepreneurs, executives, and business owners in the world – helping them stay on track, focused, and moving forward.

*"McLean International is the best thing I have ever brought into my business in my 22 years of selling, buying, and managing real estate."*

**P. Kearns-Davis,** *Columbus, OH*

You state the goal. We make sure you get there faster and easier.

Because, let's face it, it can be terribly overwhelming trying to figure out how you'll manage it all, where to start, or what your next step should be.

Been there, done that?

If you're like most entrepreneurs and business leaders, you've probably spent thousands of dollars already – hiring specialists, attending seminars, and learning new programs. But, at the end of the day, you're still wondering…

"Why haven't I achieved more in my business?"

Chances are it's because most of those so-called "solutions" used a one-size-fits-all approach. And although it might have resulted in a few steps forward initially, a cookie-cutter approach soon "hits the wall," reaching the limit of what it can do for you.

But YOUR business systems, YOUR team dynamics, and YOUR obstacles need a real solution custom-tailored to YOUR situation! And that's precisely what you get with personalized coaching from McLean International.

Choose intensive VIP days (available in half-day, full-day, and two-day options) where you (and often your team) get face-to-face with your coach, and which give you a chance to learn it where you'll use it, to one-on-one telephone coaching (for ongoing planning, action, and accountability) to our flagship program – the ultra-exclusive, limited-enrollment Elite Circle Program.

Our clients have discovered a variety of powerful ways McLean International keeps them growing:

- By getting one client's team working in a single direction, they increased sales by 26% ($8.6 million) within the first year.

- Another client increased sales revenue by 53% the first year from the business clarity and focus we provided.

- Wowed by their results, an impressive 96.5% of our clients refer other businesses to us worldwide.

We analyze your dynamics, implement systems, create a plan, monitor your systems, tweak each as needed, monitor your people, and continue making adjustments to maintain growth and profits.

It's all about responsive team coaching for the biggest gains possible. Not time management, but task management.

When you work with us, you're never pigeonholed to a single coach. Instead, you have the powerful flexibility to work with one coach or multiple coaches. Or you can transition from one coach to another as your needs change – all this because we want you to achieve the most significant gains possible as easily and quickly as you can.

**Balance Is Important!**

We believe your business and personal life should always exist in balance for ultimate success and happiness. And any improvement you make in your business should also compliment your home life. After all, your business really should exist to facilitate you enjoying the life of your dreams! (Isn't that why you went into business in the first place?)

So business and life planning must go hand-in-hand; neither one exists in a vacuum. But when you're in the thick of working IN your business, identifying where and how to make those balanced improvements can be difficult.

That's why, during your coaching sessions with us, you learn how to work ON your business not in it. You only focus on actions aimed at achieving your goals. And you'll know how to spend time only on tasks that work, while avoiding distractions. As a result, you'll enjoy faster and more significant change – and never at the expense of other things that are also important to you!

So, knowing everything's interrelated this way, we'll review your TOTAL picture to see where you are compared to where you want to be:

- Your business: We analyze the eight critical facets of your business ranging from financials to operations. You'll identify what's working, what's not working, and how to fix it.

- Your mind: Because your thinking creates results, we address subconscious obstacles that may be sabotaging your success.

- Your personal life: Do you want to leave the office by 5 p.m.? Avoid working when you're home? Have time to exercise regularly?

From this total picture, we (meaning us AND you) then drill down to the most strategic action steps available. This helps you create significant changes that are supported by all areas of your business – all while enjoying a more balanced personal life too.

If you have goals and dreams, whether they involve making more money, freeing up more time to spend with those you love, doing what you love, pouring your heart and energy into a worthwhile philanthropic cause, or perhaps even writing a book…

**WHATEVER you want,** that your current course of action isn't getting you… **we can help.**

For a more detailed look at what McLean International's coaching can do for your business and personal life, I encourage you to schedule a complimentary, no-pressure discussion of your needs today.

Just call **775-851-8934** or write to us here:
**Info@McLeanInternational.com.**

**And now listen to what other people are saying about how McLean International has helped them…**

*"Amazing! In just a few calls, you have helped us take what seemed an overwhelming task of organizing our business and helped us break it down into manageable steps. We're more organized and intentional in our daily activities and as a result, more efficient. Thanks for helping us see the forest despite the trees."*

**Lisa and Graham MacKenzie,** *Boise, ID*

*"After only two years of coaching with McLean, it's hard to believe how much progress we've made. My coach has taken my business and me from an independent lone-wolf operation to a healthy and thriving team environment. And we've experienced a 258% rate of growth since day one of coaching. But the most rewarding part has been the new energy and excitement brought to my business! Had it not been for my coach's encouragement and experience, I'm sure I would have never taken my business to the Next Level. Thank you!"*

**Cory Dudley,** *Longmont, CO*

*"From the moment our first onsite visit began, I knew that choosing to work with Linda and her team at McLean International was one of the best business decisions I've made. I now have the plan I need to grow my team and business in the right direction."*

**Lauretta Stewart,** *Toronto, ON*

*"Totally transformed my business… and my life."*

**Jane Ordway,** *New York City, NY*

*"After spending only 30 minutes together, you saved me $2,500! You've helped me look at my business from a different perspective and discover the importance of effective planning and purposeful implementation."*

**Jean Gross,** *Exton, PA*

*"In 7-1/2 months I've earned all of what I earned last year, PLUS I now have a cash reserve in the bank for my company and I'm taking a regular salary – NEVER done all that before. Coaching has been hands-down the best decision and investment I have made in business. The value of having an experienced coach that not only holds me accountable to reaching my Next Level, but also has amazing resources that help me get to where I want to go, is priceless."*

**Greg Taylor,** *Louisville, KY*

*"Is coaching a good investment? I had a 203.3% increase in my net income in one year – you tell me."*

**Dave Brenton,** *Indianapolis, IN*

www.ingramcontent.com/pod-product-compliance
Lightning Source LLC
Chambersburg PA
CBHW060316220326
41598CB00027B/4341